RIBALDRY
OF ANCIENT ROME

To HARRY CHAPLIN

The battle-cries are brushed away,
the trumpets of the grandeurs fail,
but the light kisses kissed that day
forever stay
in careless songs blown warmly by.
And we can see the lover pale
and we can hear the lover sigh.

In a lost land called Youth they dwell,
come closer as the night grows late
and laughter casts a deepening spell
and all is well:
the earth a clear eternal thing.
And we can see the lovers mate
and we can hear the lovers sing.

Catullus moaned beside me, daft,
spilling his beer, on many an eve;
with bitter wit Petronius laughed
at the world's craft
of money-values and abstract art.
These Romans in our heartbeats live
and in our dreams they play their part.

Jack Lindsay

RIBALDRY OF ANCIENT ROME

An Intimate Portrait
of Romans in Love

Edited and translated by
JACK LINDSAY

FREDERICK UNGAR PUBLISHING CO.
NEW YORK

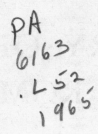

© 1961, 1965 by Jack Lindsay

Printed in the United States of America

Library of Congress Catalog Card No. 65-16614

CONTENTS

5

FOREWORD

An alternative title of this book could simply be *Romans in Love*; for under the term of Ribaldry I consider that one has the right to gather all the cheerful, delighted, and entertaining comments on, or accounts of, love-making. And the Romans on the whole remained cheerful in love, recounting even quarrels and disasters with a wry humorous note. Against this attitude we must indeed set many of the poems by Catullus, which are anguished and pathetic. But even there we find a vituperative note liable to intrude, which in its way is another version of ribaldry. (The *Concise Oxford Dictionary* describes a ribald, among other things, as an irreverent jester, user of scurrilous language. And this aspect is something we must not forget. After all, in great periods of literature, where there is a strong popular basis, there is always an outburst of that rhapsodic scurrility, which in its way is an enjoyment of language for language's sake, for its power to create an enhanced and even ecstatic image of life and people.) *Vituperatio* still had something of a magical force even in the Roman days of a highly sophisticated literature. By building up an hilarious caricature you did something to turn your enemy into the ridiculous image you had created; and so vituperation played a large part in political exchanges (e.g. item 66 here). Also, in my wish to make an all-round picture of the Romans in Love, I have included the six little poems by Sulpicia, a girl of the Tibullus circle, which have charm and pathos, and one moment of grand scorn, but which hardly come under any definition of ribaldry; here is one of the chance-survivals of a voice speaking directly out of life rather than out of literature. For the direct voice there are also the wall-scribblings from Pompeii, which give us unique glimpses of everyday life in the ancient world. Scribblers who could not have expected an audience wider than a few curious local folk have had their ephemeral notes embalmed for all time by the Vesuvian eruption.

However, Catullus and the elegists – Tibullus, Propertius, Ovid – have left us a very complete and amusing picture of the lover's life in the days of the late Republic and the early Empire, the days of Rome's greatest vitality. And though, as everywhere in Roman culture, there were derivations from the Greeks, here was one of the few points where the Romans did add something all their own. Except for Catullus, the Roman poets did not achieve great love-poetry, poetry of a rarefied and intense quality; but they did develop expansively the theme of love in its everyday delights and griefs, its humours and mishaps. The poet learned how to write about himself in a new and uninhibited way.

We have only a fragmentary section of either ancient Greek or Latin literature of the upper levels. Of the popular levels we have almost nothing. But there are enough indications to prove that the popular literature, especially on the stage, had many virtues and dealt with common life in its fullness. The love-elegies and lyrics have their points of contact with the popular level of the mimes and farces and comedies of all sorts; and there were also two great works of prose – the *Satyricon* of Petronius and the *Golden Ass* of Apuleius – which, though of a high intellectual quality, also had their roots in the lively world of popular culture.

These are the sources on which one must mainly draw for the picture of the Romans in the obsessed business of love-making in all its comedic richness. In contemplating the selection I have here made I am struck, as usual, with the extraordinary modernity of the Romans. Even the people of so recent a period as our seventeenth century seem remote when set next to the Romans of two thousand years ago. This modernity certainly derives in large part from the urban nature of Roman civilization, with all its sophistication, detachment, and subtle perspectives of self-consciousness. Anyway, here are the Romans in Love, speaking in voices that for the most part sound far more contemporary than the voices we hear on radio or television.

The period covered is some eight hundred years. Naevius, the earliest poet here represented, was born about 270 B.C. and died in 199; he may be called the founder of Roman literature: a vigorous character who clashed with the nobles. His picture of the 'Girl from Tarentum' is a fragment from a play of that name. Plautus, c. 254–184 B.C., in lively fashion merged Greek comedy into Italic elements, and Lucilius, 180–102 B.C., was, like Naevius, an outspoken character in days of violent change. Early lyric poets are represented by the passage from Aulus Gellius (90). In the late Republican days we meet a turbulent poet once more in Catullus; Caelius Rufus seems to be the man who supplanted him with his beloved Clodia; Cicero was a liberal-conservative politician of this epoch; and Laberius, from whom a tag is given, was a mime-writer who dared to pronounce, with Caesar in the audience, the line: 'He must fear many whom so many fear.'

The early days of the Empire are represented by the elegists who follow more amiably on Catullus' trail – Tibullus, Propertius, Ovid – and by Horace, lyrist and satirist. The *Barmaid* (54) used to be attributed to Virgil; it belongs to this period. The middle and the later part of the first century A.D. are represented by Martial,

Petronius, Seneca, the powerful satirist Juvenal with his gallery of bad women, and the anons of Pompeii. The second century, by Apuleius and the literary man, Aulus Gellius. To the third century we can probably attribute *The Vigil of Venus*; to the fourth century belongs Ausonius, with the Egyptian Claudian writing round the century's turn; the North-African poets, Tuccianus, Octavianus, Luxorius, carry on into the fifth and sixth centuries.

Jack Lindsay.

1. PREFATORY COUNTER-ATTACK

Martial

I F any man is so scrupulously morose that it is wrong to address him on the page of a book in the language that he speaks every day, he had been content himself with this preface and go no farther – or better still, stop at the title-page.

Epigrams are written for people who are used to watching the strip-tease Games of Flora. Let no Cato enter my Theatre – or if he enters, let him sit in peace while the show goes on. In my opinion I am keeping within my rights if I end these prefatory remarks with a little rhyming questionnaire:

> You knew, stern Cato,
> > the delightful rites
> of lewd bright Flora
> > and the rude nude rout.
> Why then did you intrude
> > upon the sights?
> Did you but come in
> > that you might go out?

2. AGAINST THE CRITICS

Catullus

Aurelius, down! you'll knuckle under!
Furius, up! I'll prove your blunder!
For I'm a shameless chap, you say,
because I like my poems gay.

The poet can't be chaste enough,
but verse is made of different stuff.
It owns no art or charm, I claim,
unless it's wanton, void of shame,
and potent, too, to aid at need
old hairy dodderers spent and lame,
not sprightly lads.
                    But when you read
The Thousand Kisses that I plead,
you think my manhood's gone to seed.
I'm coming down your way. Take heed.

[*He had just published a book of poems called* The
Thousand Kisses: *see item 6 here.*]

3. DEFINITION OF CHASTITY

Martial

I've searched the whole wide town and cannot trace
one girl who turns me down and shows surprise.
As if a No were ruin and disgrace
and wickedness, no flattered girl denies.

Is none then chaste? Yes, thousands chaste and tender.
They can't refuse although they don't surrender.

4. MAKE LOVE OUT OF DOORS

Apuleius

A WIFE is married under better auspices, with regard
to the fruitfulness of her womb, at a country-house than
in a town, on a cropping soil than in a spot of barren
dust, on the living earth than amid the stones of the
city-centre. The woman destined for motherhood should
discard her maidenhead in the very bosom of the
Mother, among the ripening corn-ears, on the sod of
fertility; or she should lie under the wedded elm, on
the lap of mother-earth, amid the childing grass, the
babies of the vine, the scions of the trees.

In harmony with this line of argument goes the line
you so often meet in our comic writers: 'Legitimate
are all babes got out of doors.'

5. SUSCEPTIBILITY

Propertius

You know, Demophoon, that yesterday
I looked at many girls, in fact at girls everywhere,
and everyone I loved. And you know also
that I consequently get into much trouble.

If I enter a street and walk along,
I'm sure to come out the other end in love.
And the theatres! they were opened to finish me off:
I'm in love again
if a girl lifts her arms, white arms tenderly outspread,
or sings and is made lovely with a song.

You want to know, Demophoon,
why any girl can catch my eye.
Love has never heard
that silly word Why.

Some men slash their arms with holy knives
or cut themselves upon the thigh
at the goading of the Phrygian flutes –
apparently they like it.

We've all madness
somewhere in us awry,
and in my case
it's wanting an infinity of wives.

Though I go blind with minstrel Thamyras, my
   grudging friend,
I'll keep my eye for beautiful girls till the very end.

6. A DAZE OF KISSES

Catullus

Quick, Lesbia, let us live and love.
At a brass farthing let us reckon
the talk of old morose-eyed men.
Suns sink, and burn again above.
With us, when the brief light is broken,
there's one long night and sleep that's blind.

Give me a thousand kisses then,
a hundred, thousand, hundred more,
and then a thousand from your store,
a hundred, till in kissing-maze
we lose our counting in a daze
and cheat malicious men who find
their wondering envy flag behind.

*   *   *

So, Lesbia, you would ask of me
How many kisses I require.
How many are poured the Libyan sands
along Cyrene's mastic shore
from where Jove's sweltering altar stands
to Battus' sacred mortuary?
How many stars, when husht is night,
look on the secret loves of men?

Kiss me those kisses, I implore,
and calm Catullus' hunger then.
The jealously counting tongues would tire
and find no potent spell of spite.

7. IN DEFENCE OF PLAIN LANGUAGE

Petronius

I FELT hot all over at the thought that I had descended so low as to bandy abuse with a part of myself which men of a more dignified type generally refuse even to recognize. I rubbed my forehead for a while, then I asked myself, 'After all, what harm have I done if I have lightened my pangs with a natural enough outburst? Isn't it a fact that we often damn this or that part of ourselves – our guts, our throat, even our heads, if they become a nuisance? Didn't Ulysses carry on an argument with his heart and didn't some tragedians damn their eyes as if eyes had ears to hear? Gouty old men swear at their feet, rheumatic persons at their fingers, shortsighted ones at their eyes; and if we have often stubbed our toes, we blame our feet for all our sufferings.

What's this, you moralist
        who scowl at me,
you'll damn my work
        of novel simplicity?
Cheerful and friendly, merry,
        pure and true,
my cleanly tongue
        but tells what people do.

Who has not happily lain
        with Venus spread?
and who denies
        that warmth to any bed?

Love is man's meaning. That's
                    the hypothesis
of Epicurus.
                    Wisdom is a kiss.

Nothing is more dishonest than a stupid moral convic-
tion; nothing more stupid than a pseudo-morality.

8. CONFESSION

Ovid

I would not presume to defend my faulty morals
or put up a phoney case for my frailties,
I confess them all
if there's any use in confessing one's errors;
and now, having made the confession,
I proceed like a fool to my own accusation.
I disapprove of what I am;
but wishing doesn't help, I'm still what I disapprove.
It's hard to endure a fate you'd like to drop,
but what can I do when I lack all self-control?
A ship is whirled off by the rapid tide,
and I'm whirled off.

No single style of beauty burns me up.
There's always a hundred causes for love about me.
Look at that girl there with her cast-down modest
    glance:
she burns me up, her modesty ensnares me.
Look at that girl pushing her bosom forward:
I'm charmed because there's nothing coy in her eye-
    brows,
her lively gestures raise my expectations.
Look at that prudish piece as stiff and gawky
as something out of ancient history:
I feel at once she wants to give herself
but hides it under a scowl of stately pride.
Look at that literary lady:

she's brimful of the most unusual tastes.
Look at that stupid creature:
isn't she charming in her simplicity?

If a girl praises my poems above the classics,
she pleases me because I'm pleasing her.
If a girl damns me utterly with my poems,
I want her at once, abusive, on my knee.
If she walks down the street with a leisurely waggle,
I'm quite enchanted with her supple curves.
If she's a waddler, if she's bandy-legged,
I imagine how gentle and graceful she'll become
after a little loving.

Here's a sweet singer, who modulates her voice
with such an ease, I want to kiss her mouth
as she is singing.
There's one whose nimble fingers stray across the
    strings
and makes them moan with sweetness,
who wouldn't want a girl with hands so skilled?
Here's one who pleases with her lovely gestures,
moving her arms in time, moving her heavy flanks
lightly in languishing dances:
the coldest fellow vowed to chastity
would wake with stings of heat at such a sight,
let alone such inflammables as I.
That girl is tall,
a heroine from the ungainly past,
filling the whole broad couch with giant charms.
This one is short and all the sprightlier.
I want them both. I want the tall and the short.
I want the uncosmeticked. I think at once
what fun to paint her and how nice she'd look.

I want the decked-out girl. She knows her value
and how to make the most of it.
I want the blonde. And the brunette as well.
A swarthy Venus is a Venus still.
Does black hair tumble on a neck of snow?
Leda was lovely with her raven tresses.
Is the hair flaxen? With her locks of saffron
how captivating was Aurora.
I find a good old legend to cap each type.
A young girl's admirable in her youth.
An older woman in knowledgeable matureness.
One wins, hands down, with looks,
the other knocks her out in wit.

In short,
there's no girl loved by anyone in all Rome
whom I don't also love and hope to gain.

9. DEFENCE-SPEECH AGAINST A LADY ACCUSING A LOVER WHO LEFT HER OF VARIOUS CRIMES

Cicero

Now, woman, if you are thinking you'll get us to approve of what you're doing, what you're saying, what you're bringing up as accusations, and what you aim at and what you want to achieve by this law-suit, you must give an intelligible and satisfying account of your close intimacy, your bosom-connexion, your surprising union with the man. The charge has a lot to say about lusts and loves and adulteries and the seaside resort Baiae and doings on the seashore and dinner-parties and revels and songs and music-parties and water-parties; and it is intimated that these matters are not brought up without your consent. And so, since through some unbridled and uncontrollable fury, which I cannot comprehend, you have chosen to cite these things in court and have them dilated on at this trial, you must either efface the charges yourself and show them baseless, or else you must admit that no credit is to be attached to any accusations you make or any evidence you may offer.

But if you wish me to deal more politely with you, I'll approach the subject along these lines. I won't summon up the ghost of your harsh and famous ancestor, an almost churlish old gentleman. No, out of the kinsmen of yours present I'll select someone else – and first of all I'll pick out your youngest brother, who is one of the best-bred men of his class, who is remarkably fond of you, and who, because of some childish timidity, I suppose – some silly fears of what may happen by night – has always since he was a little boy slept with you his eldest sister.

Suppose then that he speaks to you in these words: 'What are you kicking all this rumpus up for, sis? why are you so dotty?

'Why with such tumult do you loudly exalt
such trifles into things of mighty portent?

You saw a young chap move in as your neighbour. His fair complexion, his tall stature, his looks and his eyes tickled your fancy. You wanted to see more of him, and oftener. You were glimpsed now and then in the same gardens with him, a woman of the highest rank as you are. Yet, for all your wealth, you couldn't get him to stick to you. Not even with the thrifty scrimping old dad he's got. He kicks, he rejects you, he doesn't think your presents are worth what he's expected to do for them. All right, try someone else. You've got gardens on the Tiber. You know you had them specially made so you can overlook the spot where the lads of the town come to strip and dip. Not a day passes but you can have an eyeful and put your finger on just the lad to serve and suit you. Why rub up the wrong way this one chap who can't abide you?'

Now I've got a word to say to you, Caelius, and I'll assume the authority and strictness of a father. Not that I'm quite sure which father's part to play. Shall I take on the role of father from one of Caecilius' plays, a hardhearted and vehement old fellow?

For now at last indeed my bosom is glowing,
my heart raging with passion—

24

or that other father with his indignation:

O my unhappy son, my worthless one.

A harsh lot of fathers they are, I must say.

What shall I say, what vows may I yet form,
when your dark actions frustrate all my prayers?

A father like that would say things you wouldn't like to hear. He'd say: 'Why on earth did you find lodgings so close to a woman of low reputation? why didn't you keep out of the way of her notorious blandishments? why did you get yourself mixed up with a woman who means nothing to you? Squander your money, chuck it away, I give you leave. If you come to want, it'll be you who suffer. I shan't complain as long as I can spend agreeably my few remaining years.'

To this severe and morose old man Caelius would reply that he hadn't left the narrow path through being led astray by passion. What proof would he adduce in support of such an answer? Why, that he had been at no expense, no loss. That he hadn't fallen into the least debt.

All the same there were rumours that he had borrowed money. But how few persons can avoid that sort of report in a city so given to malicious gossip? Do you wonder that the man living next door to such a woman had his share of scandalous comment when her own brother can't escape being made a joke among the bandiers of bawdy?

So, to a kindly and considerate father such as his, who would ask, 'Has he broken the doors in? Then they shall be mended. Has he torn the girl's clothes? Then they'll be mended' – the son's cause is easily explained. For what has happened that he cannot quite simply show as in no way shadowing himself?

Don't take me up as saying something rude about that woman. Just imagine that it was a question of a woman totally unlike her – a woman who was open to anyone who came along, a woman who always had someone or other as her openly avowed lover, a woman to whose gardens, to whose house, to whose bathrooms the desires of everyone had free access as of their own right, a woman who even kept young men and made up for their fathers' meanness by her liberality – if she lived as a widow with freedom and as a wanton with lasciviousness and as a wealthy person with extravagance and as a lustful lady with all the manners of a whore, am I then to brand as an adulterer any man who may happen to salute her with a slightly unconventional liberty?

Does not, you may ask, the taking of next-door lodgings mean anything? and the things that everyone was whispering about the pair of them? Did not even Baiae blab things out rather obviously? Indeed, one can hardly talk of a mere blabbing; it was a matter of a loud shout. The circumstances proclaimed that the itch of this woman is so rash and insatiable that, not only does she ignore solitude and darkness and the normal paraphernalia of lewdness, she even exults, amidst the most unblushing behaviour, in the presence of a large crowd of onlookers – and that in the broadest daylight.

Maybe there are those among you who hold that young men are wholly forbidden all amours with courtesans. If there is any such, he is certainly a very staid and proper person. I cannot deny his moral argument; but all the same he is at odds, not only with the careless licence of today, but even with the manners of our ancestors and with their notion of what was permissible. Can anyone tell me a time when men didn't go on in that sort of way? when such gallivanting was prohibited or found fault with? when, in short, was the time when that which is lawful was not lawful? And so I'll lay down what I consider a general rule, and leave the whole thing open for each of you to apply as he pleases.

If any woman, without a husband, has thrown her house wide open to the passions of each and every man, and has openly adopted a whore's way of life, and has been accustomed to accept dinner-invitations from men with whom she is in no way related; if she does all that in the City, in country-houses, and in that most crowded of resorts, Baiae — if, in a word, she behaves in such a way, not only by her style of walking, her manner of dress, and the sort of people who throng about her — and not only by the come-hither glances of her eyes and the looseness of her conversation, but also by embracing men and kissing them at water-parties and sailing-parties and dinners, so as to give the effect not merely of a whore, but of a particularly lascivious and accomplished whore — I ask you, if a young man should happen to be seen with her, is he to be called an adulterer or a lover? does he seem to have been attacking chastity or simply to have taken an easy and well-trodden track to he easing of his desires?

Now, Clodia, you are free to suppose that what I have just said was not about you. But I ask you personally, since the accusers say they derived the idea of the charge from you and have you as a witness of its truth — I ask you, I say, if there be any woman of the sort I've sketched, a woman unlike you, a woman of the habits and profession of a tart, doesn't it appear an act of astonishing baseness and villainy for a young man to get into bed with her? If you are not such a woman — and I'd rather believe that you're not — then what are they trying to fix on Caelius? And if they try to paint you in the

27

colours of such a woman, then why need Caelius fear to be accused of the very thing you contemptuously attribute to yourself?

Give us then a line and a plan of defence. Either your modesty does it for us and declares that nothing has been done by M. Caelius with any impropriety – or else your impudence affords both him and everyone else the greatest of facilities in self-defence.

[*Clodia, of the highborn Claudian family, was the woman whom Catullus celebrated as Lesbia (items 2, 6, 76, 83). M. Caelius (see items 15, 29) supplanted Catullus, and after quarrelling with Clodia was embroiled by her in a charge of complicity in the murder of the Alexandrian ambassador. Cicero defended him and won an acquittal. The brother was Publius Clodius, a firebrand of the period, from whom Caelius had rented a house on the Palatine Hill next to Clodia's house. She was now the widow of Metellus, to whom Catullus refers in item 83. For Clodia, see 79.*]

10. TO A GIRL WELL-LOST

Horace

What slender youth now leans to kiss you, brave
with glistening odours, on a rose-strewn bed,
      Pyrrha, in some cool cave?
    For whom is dressed your yellow head

so neatly exquisite? O, long he'll weep
for faith and gods estranged, and shrink to see
      the black winds lash the deep
    which smiled on him so placidly.

Ah, golden is the girl he fondly clasps.
He thinks her always fancyfree and kind.
      The wind that roars and rasps
    is yet unknown. Poor men and blind

for whom untried you gleam. The sailors' shrine
shows grateful tablets hung aloft by me
      and garments soaked in brine
    vowed to the god who rules the sea.

11. AGAINST A SEA VOYAGE

Ovid

CORRINA is abandoning the bed she knows so well,
abandoning the shrines of her home, and getting ready

to go on a sailing trip. Why, on your behalf, must I shiver at the thought of all the winds of the compass, east west north and south? You won't see any cities to admire, any groves for a love-tryst. Nothing but the monotonous blue of the treacherous waters.

You won't see any little shells out in mid-sea. Any tinted pebbles. Those are the things you find to make you dawdle on the sandy shore. The shore is the only place for lovely girls to tread with their marble feet. That's safe enough. Everything else is thick with hazards.

After you've sailed out for a while, the land disappears. The cable's been cast off and the curved ship dips out into the boundless main where the worried sailor fears the winds of storm and sees death hovering as near as the restless waves. What if Triton stirs up the agitated waters? Then we'll see how quick the colour leaves your face. Then you'll call upon the saviour-stars and cry out, 'How happy is the girl who comes to her haven of land! It's nicer to lie snugly abed, read entertaining books, and pluck the strings of the lyre!'

I'll be the first on the shore of Baiae to see the familiar ship. I'll shout, 'It's the one that carries my life!' And I'll welcome you into my arms and snatch indiscriminate kiss upon kiss. The victim vowed for your return will bleed, and the soft sand be heaped as a table for us. Then, with the wine poured out, you shall tell me many a tale – how your boat nearly went under and how while you were hurrying along to me you didn't fear the dangerous night-hours or the gusty southern gales. Though there isn't a word of truth in it all, I'll fervently believe.

12. BRING MONEY

Tibullus

Thin Coan stuffs and lustrous Red-Sea pearls
awoke an appetite unsatisfied.
Doors slyly creaked and wicked grew our girls
and on the threshold wakeful dogs were tied.

Bring money. Then the doors unbar with speed,
dogs wag their tails, the guardians turn to bless.
The god who made a lovely girl feel greed
mixed one good thing with varied viciousness.

Therefore our joys are angry, sad, and rash,
and on the earth Love roams with godhead stained.
But you who shut your lovers out for cash –
may fire and sword reclaim the gold you've gained.
Young men will watch your house burned down to
  ash,
they'll watch it burn unquencht, with joy unfeigned.

31

13. A COSTLY GIRL

Aulus Gellius

SOTION was a philosopher of the Peripatetic School, far from an obscure position. He wrote a book full of wide and varied information, and entitled it *The Horn of Plenty*.

In it he tells the following anecdote about the orator Demosthenes and the courtesan Lais. 'Lais of Corinth,' he remarks, 'used to gain a great deal of money through the grace and charm of her body, and had a constant stream of visiting by rich men from all over Greece. But she never let any of them in until they handed over whatever she demanded, and her demands were extravagant enough.'

He adds that thus arose the proverb, common among the Greeks, 'Not every man can fare to Corinth town.' For it was useless for anyone to go to Corinth and call on Lais unless he was able to pay her price.

'The great Demosthenes made overtures to her behind the scenes and asked for the favour of an embrace. But she demanded 10,000 drachmas down' – a sum equivalent in our money to 10,000 denars. 'Amazed and shocked at the woman's immeasurable impudence and the huge sum of money she asked, he turned away, remarking as he left her, "I won't buy regret at so high a price." ' The witticism goes more neatly in the Greek.

[*The average wage of a daily labourer was about one drachma or denarius.*]

14. THE LOVER AT THE RACES

Ovid

O, it's no thoroughbred horse I come to see.
The horse you favour is the horse for me.
I come to talk and sit with you awhile
and thrust my love upon your wounding smile.
You watch the horses while I'm watching you.
I wish us both a satisfying view.

Why do you shrink? We're close and can't withdraw,
for at the Circus that's the benching law.
But easier! you fellow on the right!
you're hurting her, you're squeezing in so tight.
And you behind, don't make your leg so free,
for shame don't press her back with bony knee.

Look, girl, and see your skirts, how loose they lie.
Lift them, or don't object if I should try.
O enemy skirt, to hide such legs from me!
In lifting, skirt, you're still my enemy.
I loved before I saw. Then what's the game?
Water for ocean, flame to feed a flame!
From that one piece the rest I can surmise,
that hidden finely from my questing eyes.

Meanwhile please stir your hand or shake your fan
and sway some coolness on a suffering man.
O, is it blood or sun? I feel distressed.
O, is it woman's love that burns my breast?

But while I speak, some dust comes sprinkling by.
Don't touch her limbs of snow, foul dust, I cry.
Hey, the procession! Come, let's give our cheers.
Come, fellows, shout. The gold procession nears.
First, with her wings outspread, comes Victory.
(Be kind, O goddess, hand this girl to me.)
Lovers of ships, give Neptune now your voice,
(I don't like waves. The earth's my better choice.)
Soldiers, cry out for Mars. (But dumb am I.
Peace I desire, where Love can safely lie.)
Phoebus for priests, for hunters Phoebe stands.
Minerva blesses the creative hands.
Farmers, hail Ceres or the God of Wine.
Boxers and Jockeys, hail the Twins Divine.
(You, gentle Venus with the Lad that flies
to pierce our heart, O aid my enterprise.
Yes, make my new girl ready to be mine . . .
I saw her nod, she gave the favouring sign.)
Girl, promise what the goddess promised me:
by Venus' leave, then more divine you'll be.
I swear by all the Gods now trooping by,
I'll be your faithful lover till I die.
But look, your legs hang down. To watch the shows
in comfort, on the railing rest your toes.

The space is clear. The umpire signs. They start.
Out past the bar the four-hourse chariots dart.
I see your choice. He'll win, he'll win, I swear!
for of your will the horses seem aware.
He swings too widely round the turning-place.
He should have hugged the stone. He'll lose the race.
You wretch, she'll never pick you out again.
Hey, take a grip and tighten your left rein.
The fool! Here, Romans, hoot him out of town.
Let each spectator shake a scornful gown.

They're coming back. The people push and tear.
Lean close against me, just to save your hair.
Now once again they've opened up the course.
The spangled riders come. I see his horse.
Outrun them all! O gain and keep the lead!
Praying that you will grant her prayer, I plead.

She has her wish, but mine remains a thought.
She has her palm, but mine must still be sought.
Quick eyes have spoken in her smiling face.
Enough! The rest can wait a fitter place.

15. GOSSIP

M. Caelius Rufus

NOTHING new whatever at all has happened – unless you want me to send such gossip as follows, and I'm sure you do.

Young Cornificius is engaged to Orestilla's daughter.

Paulla Valeria, sister of Triarius, has divorced her husband without explanation on the very day he returned home from governing his province. She is marrying Decimus Brutus. She has sent him back her entire wardrobe.

Many incredible things of this sort have kept on happening in your absence. Servius Ocella would never have persuaded anyone in the world that he ever succeeded in seducing anything, if he hadn't been caught twice in the act in three days. You'll ask, 'Where?' The very last place, on my word, that I could have wished. I leave you something to drag out of the others. For I find it amusing that a General should pester people

with questions as to who the lady was on top of whom
someone was surprised.

[*He is writing to Cicero, who has been governing a
province and so is a general.*]

16. INVITATION

Catullus

So please the gods, soon at my home
as well as anywhere at Rome,
Fabullus, you will nobly dine
if you'll but bring good food along,
a pretty wench, some wit, some wine,
and lots and lots of jest and song.
Then you'll dine well; for things get worse,
I've only cobwebs in my purse.

But love I'll serve with all my will
and something neater, sweeter still.
For Venus and her Cupids lent
this Essence as my girl's own scent.
Approach, and you'll forget your woes,
praying to be entirely Nose.

17. NOON SURPRISE

Ovid

IT happened in the summer. Noon had just gone by when I dropped in a sprawl on the couch, hoping to feel refreshed. The window was partly thrown open, partly shuttered, and the light had a forest-glimmer about it, a sort of twilight softness that one finds after sunset or early in the morning, just before the sun comes up. No better light for a shy girl who wants to show herself and yet to feel modest at the same time.

And there was Corinna, clothed in a loose frock, with her hair let down over her white neck: just the way that Queen Semiramis used to enter her bedroom, or that Lais whom many a hero embraced. I pulled the frock aside, a frail thing it was, hardly worth mentioning, and yet she struggled to keep it on. Still, she didn't fight as though she were very anxious to win; and so, betraying herself, she was easily beaten. She stood before me without a veil, and I couldn't detect the least flaw in her scrutinied beauty. What shoulders, what arms I saw and fondled, what finely contoured breasts, and below, what smoothness warmly curving. How full and lovely her flanks. How plumply young her thighs. But why make a catalogue? Every inch I saw deserved its full measure of praise. I held her close.

You know the rest. Tired at last, we lay side by side. I only wish that I often had such a midday.

18. THREE LOVE POEMS

Octavianus

Come, painter, paint my girl in all
    her wealth of warming whiteness,
the girl whom Love has painted and
    who's limned with breathing brightness.
Yes, paint her as she fully is,
    beneath a silken gown
that bares her hidden body as
    it finely ripples down.
Ah, love has shaken you as well.
    The picture's in your heart.
Then paint the sigh of your desire
    if you would show your art.

*   *   *

The flower will not bloom again,
    the lover's gain is lost
when cheaply bought; but sweet the joy
    when heavy is the cost.
O if too easily the sheets
    on beauty's bed are tossed,
the wanton heart forgets the lure,
    the lover's gain is lost.

*   *   *

O what's your way with lovers if
    they will not love again,
beautiful Venus? Head to foot,
    in time, all grace must wane.

The dew will come, but violets parch,
    the scents of roses fade;
when spring is past, the lilies doff
    their white and droop decayed.
Then take these images to heart;
    and when a lover's true,
O love him back, for still he'll love,
    if still he's loved by you.

19. THE GOOD LITTLE TART

Plautus

Philolaches (entering, rather drunk). Now there's a matter, it's long been on my mind, an argument I've been having with myself, it's been revolving in my head, I mean, if I've got one, you get my drift, I've been debating, you might say reasoning about it for a long time, as time goes, I mean, you see it's this, what the hell a man is like. You get me, when he's born, what is he? what's he like? Well, the point is that I just got it clear.

A new house. That's what I make him out. When he's born, I mean. He's like a new house. I'll explain how I got it so correct. And I know that all you people over there, when you hear what I got to say, you won't say a thing different yourselves, you'll admit I got it exactly the way I'm putting it to you. So listen while I show you just how I figure it all out. I want you to be as well up in things as what I am myself.

A new house now. As soon as it's all complete, you know, finished off, fixed up to the last bit of what-you-may-call-it, what do they do? They compliment the builder and say what a good house it is. Everybody asks the owner to let him have a copy of the plans, everyone wants the same house for himself, and he won't spare himself any cost or trouble. Just so. But when some slug of a slacker with a damn-all household, some slovenly bag of lazybones moves into that wonderful house, then the house suffers for it, being a good house still, but badly looked-after. And then it often happens that a storm blows up and smashes the tiles and the gutters. Then the damn-all owner won't do a thing to repair them. Down comes the rain, down it runs into the walls, down it oozes into them, down it rots the woodwork and ruins all the builder's hard work. And so the houses grow the worse for wear. And it's not the builder's fault at all. It's just the way that most people go on. If a thing can be mended for sixpence, they put it off and put it off, and don't do anything about it, till at last the walls crash in, and the whole place has to be rebuilt.

Well, that's enough about houses. Now I want to pass on to tell you why I think men are just like houses are. In the first place, parents are the builders of their children, eh? They lay the foundations of their children's lives. They rear 'em, do their best to get 'em into shape, solid shape, and don't think about cost-charges while they're trying to turn 'em into useful and ornamental men and citizens, eh? Money spent on all that they don't count expense. They lay on the finishing touches, teach 'em literature, jurisprudence, law, spare no cash or labour so that others may pray for their sons to be like theirs. And so, fully constructed, they send 'em into the army, now giving 'em as a sort of buttress some of their kinsmen. Well, the job's done. The lads leave the builders' hands. And after they've served a campaign, there's signs coming up as to how the building will wear and tear.

Take myself. Up to that point – while I was in the builders' hands, I was always a steady serious sort of bloke. But after I was left to my own disposition, I ruined all the work. Did it immediately and made a thorough job of it. Idleness settled down on me, and that was my storm. Coming up on me heavy with hail, beating down without a warning. It stripped me of my poor coating of modesty and morals. And after that I was too careless to put a new cover on. And, soon enough, the rain came. That was love. It went on dripping, dripping into my bosom, drenching my heart out. And I've lost everything — cash and credit, reputation, character, and good name, the whole damn lot. And myself I've become very much the worse for wear. Yes, by heaven, these timbers of mine are all soaked and rotting. And I just somehow can't get round to repairing my house in time — stop it from crashing right in and falling into everlasting ruin, foundations and all, and not a living soul can help me.

It makes me feel sick to think what I am, and what I was. Not one of our young chaps trained harder or had a better name as an athlete. Disc-throwing, spear, ball, running, fencing, riding — that was all the high life I wanted — an example of strict and simple living for the others. Why, the best lads of all tried to make me their model. And now I'm a worthless clod — but I can't complain, it's my own make-up that's done it for me.

(He stops moodily and loiters. Out of one of the houses come the girl Philematium and her old attendant Scapha. They carry on with the girl's toilet.)

Phil. Dear me, I can't remember a cold bath that I enjoyed more. I don't believe I've ever been so rubbed and scoured in all my life, Scapha.

Scapha (with a grin). Everything has its proper outcome, just as this year gave us a whopping harvest.

Phil. But what has a harvest got to do with my bath?

Scapha. No more than your bath has got to do with the harvest.

Philolaches (noticing the womenfolk). O, my lovely love, there she is — the storm that has stripped me bare of all my thin coating of modesty. Then it was that love and passion oozed into my bosom, and now I can't put the covering back, not ever. Now the walls of my heart are soaked right through and the house is a shambles.

Phil. (prinking herself). Scapha dear, do please look me over and see if this frock really suits me. I do so much want to please Philolaches, my darling, he's so good to me.

Scapha. Then why not just dress yourself up in your most charming smile, since you're so charming in yourself? It's not the frock a lover wants. It's what is inside the frock.

Philol. (aside). Lord love me, but isn't Scapha an old dear too. Such a wise old hag. The charming way she has of understanding just how lovers act and feel.

Phil. (posing). Well now?

Scapha (pretending not to follow her). Well what?

Phil. Look at me, look me over and see if this suits me.

Scapha. You're so lovely that anything suits you.

Philol. (aside). Good old girl, I'll certainly make you a present of something for those words. I'll see you get a return for praising the girl that I find so delightful.

Phil. But I don't want you to flatter me.

Scapha. You're a silly little thing then. You'd rather be abused insincerely than sincerely admired. Love-a-duck, I prefer compliments, whether or not they're meant, to a lot of sincere criticism or having folk grin at my looks, yes, indeed I do.

Phil. (quietly). I love sincerity and I want what's said of me to be sincere. I can't bear a liar.

Scapha. As you love me, pretty, and as your Philolaches loves you, I swear you're too charming to be true.

Philol. (aside). What's that, you old bitch? What sort of an oath was that? As I love her – how about as she loves me? Why not bring that in? I give-up giving that present. You've done for yourself, and done the present in too.

Scapha. But, dearie, I really am surprised you're such

a silly, you silly thing, when I know what a shrewd, biddable, well-trained girl you are and all.

Phil. O please, if I'm making a mistake, do tell me what it is.

Scapha. Mistake! I should say that isn't the word for it. Here you are, all wrapt up in that one man and thinking he's a sort of tinpot god, without as much as a sidelong glance at anyone else. To give yourself up to one lover — that's the stuff for married women, not girls that live on the game.

Philol. (aside). Good God, what monster have I turned loose in my house? May all the heavenly powers damn me to the worst horrors of hell if I don't do that old bag-of-bones to death by hunger, thirst, and cold.

Phil. Now, Scapha, I don't want any more wicked advice from you.

Scapha. O you're downright stupid, it stares you in the face, to think he'll always be loving and wanting to look after you. I warn you. He'll drop you when you're older and he cools off.

Phil. (sadly). I hope not.

Scapha. Our hopes come true less often than hope-nots. Use your brains. If words can't convince you that my words are true, then look at the facts of life. You see what I am now. But you don't see what I used to be. I was loved just as much as you are. I devoted myself to one man and no more. And he— O well, when the years came over and changed the colour of this head of mine, he went off and left me alone. It'll be the same with you, I'm sure.

Philol. (aside). I can hardly hold myself back from having a fling at her eyes, the wicked old temptress.

Phil. He spent his money to get me free, just me, and all for himself. I feel I'm doing right in keeping myself for him, and him only.

44

Philol. (aside). You gods on high, now isn't she a darling thing, with the truest heart you could find? Yes, I did a good job, I'm delighted to be a ruined man for her sake.

Scapha. Good lord, you haven't been born yet!

Phil. Why?

Scapha. Fancy being so worked up about his loving you.

Phil. Worked up? I ask you, why shouldn't I be?

Scapha. You're a free woman now. You've got what you were after. It's yours. As for him, unless he sticks to loving you, he'll have thrown into the gutter all that money he laid out on you.

Philol. (aside). I'll be damned if I don't murder that creature by every method known to man. The old bawd, trying to spoil the girl by her dirty hints and cajoleries.

Phil. I can't ever be grateful enough to him, see, never. So you stop trying to bring him down in my estimation, Scapha.

Scapha. I only want to get one idea into that head of yours. If you give yourself up to him, every bit, while you're young, you'll be sorry as hell when you're old.

Philol. (aside). O, if I could only change to a quinsy and catch that old viper in her villainous throat and throttle her.

Phil. I ought to feel just as loving, now I've got what I wanted, as when I used to coax him before.

Philol. (aside). The gods may do as they like with me if I don't set you free all over again for saying that – and if I don't settle that Scapha's hash.

Scapha. Well, if you've got a guarantee that he'll be board and lodgings for you till the end of time – your own doting lover while you've got a squeak in your body

– the thing for you to do is to put yourself at his sole disposal and have your hair done up like a bride.

Phil. One can generally get money according to the sort of name one has. If I keep a good name, I'll be rich enough.

Philol. (aside). Now, by the Lord, even if it comes to selling my father, I'll sell him up, rather than you come to want or beggary while I draw breath.

Scapha. But what'll become of all these other men in love with you?

Phil. They'll love me all the more when they see how grateful I am to my benefactor.

Philol. (aside, overjoyed). O for news now that my father's at his last gasp, so I could disinherit myself and make her heir of all the property I'm left.

Scapha. Still, it won't be long before he's used up all he's got, gorging and swilling night and day, with no one giving a moment's thought to thrift. Just sheer guzzlery, I call it.

Philol. (aside). Thrift? Yes, it's time I had a shot at it, and the first thing I'll cut down on is you. Not a thing to eat or drink shall you have in my house for the next ten days.

Phil. If you want to say something nice about him, say it. But if you go on running him down, I swear you'll have a whipping before you know where you are.

Philol. (aside). Why, if I'd made an offering of an ox to the Lord High God with the money I paid out for her, it wouldn't have been so well invested. You can see she loves me with all she's got. I congratulate myself. I freed an advocate to plead my case better than I could.

Scapha. I see you feel that no one's worth tuppence next to Philolaches. So I'd rather agree with you and not get whipped on his account.

Phil. Hand me the mirror and the jewellery-box.

46

Hurry, Scapha. I must look my best when Philolaches comes, the darling boy.

(She takes the mirror and arranges her hair.)

Scapha. Only the woman worried about her looks and her years need call on the mirror. Why do you need one? Can't you see you're the mirror's own best mirror?

Philol. (aside). You'll get your reward for such a pretty speech, Scapha. And you, Philematium dear, I'm going to start building up some capital in your name.

Phil. Is everything all right now? Please look. Is my hair done well enough?

Scapha. When you've got a pretty face, your hair is always done prettily.

Philol. (aside). Bah, do you know anything as base as that old bitch? Now her wicked tongue's all compliments, and a moment ago she was sharp and contrary.

Phil. Hand me the ceruse.

Scapha. Ceruse? what do you want that for?

Phil. To rub on my cheeks.

Scapha. You might as well expect to whiten ivory with ink.

Philol. (aside). Very neat, ivory and ink. Good on you, Scapha. Keep it up.

Phil. Then give me the rouge.

Scapha. No, I won't. You're just dotty. Wanting to smear fresh paint on a perfectly lovely picture. Girls at your age shouldn't use the least touch of colour or ceruse or Melian cream or any other cosmetic.

Phil. All right. Hold the mirror. *(She reluctantly hands the mirror back after a last look.)*

Philol. Damn it all, she's kissed the mirror. O for a stone to bash that mirror's head in.

Scapha. Take a towel and wipe your hands.

Phil. But why, please?

Scapha. (with a grin). Now you've held the mirror,

47

I'm afraid your hand will smell of silver, and Philolaches mustn't ever suspect you handle silver, must he?

Philol. (aside). I don't think I ever saw a sharper-witted old go-between. Quite smart and pointed that joke about the mirror, the dirty old so-and-so.

Phil. Surely I can sprinkle on a little scent?

Scapha. Not at all.

Phil. But why?

Scapha. Good heavens, don't you know a woman smells best when she doesn't smell at all? Look at those dried-up old things who pickle themselves in perfume, patched-up hags without a tooth in their head, who try to paint out all their bodily blemishes. As soon as their scents and their sweat mix together, they smell just like when the cook concocts a sauce-mixture. You can't tell what it is they smell of – but you know one thing, they stink.

Philol. (aside). She's no fool, that old girl. She's up to all the tricks. There never was a wiser old lady. She's right enough. *(To audience.)* Admit it, chaps. Most of you have got a lot of old wives stuck away at home, who bought you up with their dowries.

Phil. (after a last wriggle). Here now, Scapha, do look over my jewellery and frock, and see if it really, really suits me.

Scapha. But after all that's no business of mine.

Phil. If it isn't yours, whose is it then?

Scapha. Philolaches of course. So he won't buy anything but what he thinks suits himself. What's the use of showing off to him, unasked, something he doesn't want on his hands. Purple's for the old, jewels for the ugly. A pretty girl's prettier with nothing on than dressed in purple. For then she's overdressed, if she's really pretty.

Philol. (aside). I'm keeping my hands off her too long. *(He comes forward.)* What's going on here?

Phil. (rushing to embrace him). I'm just dressing up to please you.

Philol. You're dressed quite enough. *(To Scapha.)* Go on, get inside and take all that paraphernalia with you. *(Scapha ducks and nods and hurries in.)* O my darling, my dear Philematium, I'd love to have a drink with you.

Phil. And me with you. Whatever you like, I like, my darling.

Philol. Ah, that word would come cheap at a hundred pounds.

Phil. Well, give me fifty, there's a ducks. I want you to get a bargain.

Philol. (carrying on the joke). You owe me fifty still. Count it up if you like. It's a hundred and fifty I paid.

Phil. (hurt). Why do you throw it up at me?

Philol. Throw it up at you? Why, what I want is to have it thrown up at me every moment of the day. I've never made such a splendid bargain in all my short life.

Phil. And I'm sure I couldn't do anything better with my love than hand it all over to you, dearest.

Philol. Then our books balance exactly. You love me and I love you, and both of us think that's just what it should add up to. May those who are happy in our happiness, be happy themselves with an unending happiness — but as for those who envy us, I only pray that nobody will ever envy them for what's come to them.

Phil. (drawing him over to a couch). Come on then, take your place. *(Calls to a slave within.)* Some water for our hands, boy. Put a small table there. And the dice — go and find them. *(To Philolaches).* Would you like some perfume?

Philol. (embracing her). What for? with the essence of myrrh here beside me?

(Slaves come in with table and various things. Philolaches peers down the street.)

Look there. It's my pal, isn't it, rolling along with his girl? Yes, it is. It's Callidamates and his mistress on his arm. Hurray, my dearest chap. Look, the whole regiment's assembling. All our friends turning up to get a share of the loot.

(Callidamates comes in very drunk. With him is his girl Delphium and a slave.)

Call. (to the slave). I want you now on the spot come to Philolaches' place, y'know, and get me to come there on time. Prompt, see. Don't forget. Off. Got your orders. *(Slave goes and the drunk addresses nobody in particular.)* Well now I was there y'see, so I left it, just left it, ran off, damn tired, all those people there, all talking, damn tired, ran off. Now I'll drop in on my friend. Want something to drink, just a drop. Sure to be jolly, all have a good time, whoopie. *(To Delphium.)* Now would you say I was bub-bub-boozed . . . or bub-bub . . . well you know.

Del. Same as ever. *(Pulls him along.)* You're obstructing yourself. Here's the place we want.

Call. Tell you what. I'll hug you and you hug me. Good idea, eh?

Del. If you think you'd like it. Carry on.

Call. (grabbing her). You're a d'licious little something-or-other. Take my arm or you'll trip. *(He lurches and almost falls over.)*

Del. Come on now, keep on your feet. *(She takes a firm grip.)* There now, stand up.

Call. My only only only . . . I'm your baby-boy, sweety-pie.

Del. Yes, of course you are. But still I think you

oughtn't to sit down in the street. It'll be so much nicer on a soft warm couch where we lie down together.

Call. That's it . . . just let me drop.

Del. There, you've gone and made me drop my parcel. *(She pulls him up.)* If you must go falling, then you shan't fall without me falling too.

Call. It's all right. Somebody'll find us lying here . . . pick us both up after while. All right.

Del. I do believe you're drunk.

Call. (drawing himself indignantly up). You dare say I'm d-d-d-drunk?

Del. (soothingly). Come on, gimme your hand. I can't let you break your neck.

Call. Here you are. Take it.

Del. Right now. This way. Come on.

Call. Where am I going? Forget, eh?

Del. Don't you know?

Call. Course I know. Just occurred to me. Course I know. *(Brightly.)* I'm going home to get a drink.

Del. No, no, you're going there. *(She points.)*

Call. That's right. All clear now.

Philol. (to Philematium). You don't mind if I go to meet him, do you, pet? I look upon him as the best friend I've got. Back in a minute. *(He rises and goes to Callidamates.)*

Phil. A minute? It'll be hours to me.

Call. (yelling). Anyone here at home?

Philol. Just what we are.

Call. (embracing him). Good old lad! splendid. Best friend I got in whole wide world.

Philol. (guiding him to a couch). Heaven bless you. Here's your place. Where have you come from?

Call. Somewhere or other, y'know, where you get boozed.

Phil. And you too, Delphium my dear girl, why don't

you make yourself comfortable. *(To a slave.)* Give my friend a drink.

Call. (drinking the glass off). And now I'll tell you what, I'm going . . . sleep. *(Flops back and snores.)*

Philol. (to Delphium). Just behaving according to schedule, eh?

Del. O what'll I do with him now?

Phil. Just leave him where he is to sleep it off, my dear. *(To the slave.)* Come on, boy, jump to it. Take the drinks round. Delphium first.

20. A SLEEPLESS GIRL SCRIBBLES ON THE WALL

Anon.

Would I could clasp you, with small arms round your
    neck,
and press my kisses on your tender lips.
Go then, poppet, confide your joys to the winds.
Believe me, the nature of men is light.
Often I've woken in desperate depths of night
thinking things over with a sigh.
Many whom Fortune has thrust up on high
she suddenly harries, they slip and fall in pain.
So Venus, mingling the sudden bodies of lovers,
parts them again.

[*The writer of these lines on the wall of a Pompeian bedroom was obviously a girl, but at the end she has clumsily written 'One Martius,' in order to hide her tracks.*]

21. A GIRL IN LOVE

Sulpicia

Gossip, at last a love has come to me.
Veils and not naked candours I detest.
Venus, won over by my Muse's plea,
led him and laid him here upon my breast.

Her promise is fulfilled. Let whisperers frown,
who never had a lover of their own.
I'll write him notes, but scorn to seal them down
or keep my faithful thoughts for him alone.

I love my fault. No masks shall mar my face.
Worthy of one another, we embrace.

*   *   *

My birthday's near. I hate it. You in Rome,
Cerinthus – what could country-boredoms yield?
Not farms but cities are a girl's true home,
not chilly rivers in an Arretine field.

*   *   *

Rest then, my uncle, troublesomely kind.
Some journeys are inopportune, you know.
Me you may take away, but not my mind;
for here my will remains, though forced I go.

*   *   *

Have you heard your girl is rescued from distress?
In Rome now for her birthday she can stay.
Then let us join to celebrate this day
which comes by merest whim of happiness.

*   *   *

I'm glad. Your unconcern you frankly showed.
It saves me from rash slips of misery.
Then you prefer the wench with the wool-load,
the slut, to Servius' girl, Sulpicia, me.

Others are worried. Yes, their hearts have bled
that I should lose you to some nameless bed.

*   *   *

My weary body's racked with fever still,
Cerinthus. Is it nothing, dear, to you?
I would not pray to cease from lying ill
unless I thought that you were praying too.

What use would health, unfevered, prove to me
if you could watch my sufferings callously.

*   *   *

May you, my life, forget the tender truth
that's fed, these last few days, your love with flame,
if there's a single folly of my youth
which makes me shrink with such repentant shame
as that I left you yesternight alone,
afraid that all my passion might be shown.

54

[*These are the complete works of Sulpicia, who belonged to the circle of Tibullus. The latter's patron was Messalla, her uncle. She was then a girl of high birth who carried on an affair with the man whose name is masked by 'Cerinthus'. The 'wench with the wool-load' was the prostitute; note the mounting pride of the line that follows: 'the slut, to Servius' girl, Sulpicia, me'. In the few short poems there is a remarkable revelation of character.*]

22. LOVE LETTERS

Ovid

[*Some comments to the servant-girl Nape, aimed at get
ting her on his side.*]

NAPE, there's nothing you don't know about catching up a straggle of tresses and producing a first-rate
hair-do. In my opinion you're too good to be reckoned
among the slave-girls. You're well up too in all the tricky
devices of the stealthy dark, and skilled at giving the
signals. I know that when Corinna was wavering about
a visit to me, you've often pleaded with her to come.
You've been faithful to me in my troubles. So take these
tablets that I've filled so well this morning. Take them
to your mistress and with your diligence do all you can
to get rid of delays and dilly-dallyings. As for yourself,
I know you don't possess veins of stone or a bosom of un-
yielding iron in that body of yours, and you know all
that a girl of your type is liable to know. No doubt at all
that you've heard the twang of Cupid's bow as he shot
you in the necessary spots. On my behalf then raise the
banner of your service. If Corinna asks what I'm doing,
say that I'm just twiddling my thumbs in desperate ex-
pectation of nightfall. The wax over which my persua-
sive hand has scribbled will say all the rest.

But while I'm chattering on, time flies. Choose the
right occasion to give her my tablets, when she's at leisure a moment. But then make sure she reads them
through at once. I ask you to watch her eyes and her
brow as she reads; from her silent features you can make

out the future. And don't let her yawn and do nothing. As soon as she's finished reading, suggest that she writes me back a long answer. I hate a letter where the bleached wax is practically empty, with a big margin every side. Let her write her lines close together as they run on, and I'll be happy to have my eyes long kept busy with making out what she's scrawled on the extreme edge.

But after all, why does she need to cramp her fingers with gripping the pen? Her letter will be long enough if it consists of a single word: Come. Then I'd lose no time in crowning my triumphant tablets with laurel and setting them in the midst of the temple of Venus. And under them I'd inscribe:

Ovid offers his Faithful Servants
   to Venus gratefully,
though a while ago they were nothing
   but slats from a maple-tree.

*   *   *

Commiserate my bad luck. My tablets have come with sad tidings. Her ill-fated letter announces that she won't be at home today. After this I'll agree there's something in omens. As Nape was on the way out, she knocked her foot against the threshold and stopped short. My girl, when next time you're sent out of doors, remember to pass over the threshold with more care and lift your foot up like a sober woman.

But as for you, you heartless tablets, you fatal slabs of board, get off with you! and take the wax with you, crammed as it is with denying words. I feel sure that the Corsican bees from whom it comes collected their abominable honey from the flowers of the tall hemlock.

You were red, you tablets, as though you'd been well dyed in vermilion. The exact colour of blood. Useless shingles of wood, out you go into the street, and there you may lie. I hope a heavy wheel crushes you as it rumbles along. I could prove by severe logic that the man who cut you to shape from the tree lacked the hands of innocence. And the tree itself, it was used as the gibbet for some miserable neck. It has supplied the dreadful crosses for the executioner. It has provided a disgusting roost for screech-owls. In its boughs it has borne nests full of the eggs of the owls and the vultures. In my madness, have I entrusted my courtship to you? have I handed over my wooing words to be carried to my girl by such emissaries?

These tablets more fitly would have held the interminable jargon of a summons pronounced by some sour-faced judge. They ought to be chucked out to lie among diaries and daybooks, over which some whining old miser laments his squandered substance. Haven't I found you out, in fact as well as in name, a double-dealer, a two-leafed booklet, a two-faced crook? I should have known that you'd turn out of ill-omened duplicity. Well, in my rage, there's only one prayer I can make for you. May an old age of worm-eaten rottenness consume you and may your wax go fluffy-white with repellent mould!

23. THE VIGIL OF VENUS

Anon.

Love for the loveless ones tomorrow,
Love for all the lovers too!

Spring it young and Spring's a song and Spring is earth
  that's born anew,
bidding merry Loves take hands and bidding birds go
  mate again.
Trees let all their curling tresses down beneath the nuptial rain.
On the morrow She who holds the Loves embracing
  subtly weaves
greening bowers with sprays of myrtle underneath the
  shadow of leaves.
On the morrow, lofty-seated, She will tell us what to do.
  Love for the loveless ones tomorrow,
  Love for all the lovers too!

Now Dione with the flowering gems adorns the crim-
  soning Year.
All the little nipple-buds, that swell when west the winds
  appear,
widely into clusters She cajoles, then sprinkles drops of
  light –
dew that cools the earth of summer, heading from the
  breath of night.
Quivering gleams the teardrop as it pulls and gathers all
  its strength

and the tiny globe of light lets go and slithers down at
length.
Dew which quiet pulsing stars distil when clouds are
blown away
soothes the maiden paps from wetted shifts to greet the
break of day.
Blossoms tremulously blush to stand with all their veils
withdrawn,
for the Goddess bade each virgin rose to marry in the
dawn.
Out of Venus-bloodshed and the kiss of Love their hues
were won,
out of gems, and out of flames, and out of crimson of the
Sun.
Closely veiled inside her burning sheath remains each
secret bride:
on the morrow she will tear her shift and show the
warmth inside.

> *Love for the loveless ones tomorrow,*
> *Love for all the lovers too.*

Venus has despatched her maids as calm and virginal as
you:
'Only one request, we bring. Retire, we beg you, Delian
Maid.
Let no blood of forest-beasts be dabbled on the peaceful
shade.
Venus would have come in person if a chasteness she
might sway.
Venus would have asked your presence, but you'd scorn
to share our play.
Now for three long festal nights you'll see the bands of
laughter rove
trespassing with mingled merriments along each ringing
grove.

Bright amid the garlands of the flowers, the bowers of
   myrtle green.
Ceres smiling with red Bacchus and the God of Poets
   will be seen.
All the night the revelry will wake and songs will rouse
   desire,
and Dione then will rule the world. So, Delian Maid,
   retire.'
   Love for the loveless ones tomorrow,
   Love for all the lovers too.

High among the flowers of Hybla Venus sets her judge-
   ment-seat.
With the Graces at her side, the Laws of Love she'll
   there repeat,
Hybla, pour your flowers out, O all the blooms that
   summer yields.
Hybla, don your dress of flowers through the whole of
   Hybla's fields,
so that She may see on youngster-buds her refreshing
   shadow fall.
Girls of Meadow, Girls of Hill, they all obey the happy
   call.
Girls of Forest, Girls of Glen, the gathering Girls of
   Spring obey.
For the Mother of the Lad with Wings has named the
   meeting-day,
warning us that even naked Love can cause a girl to rue.
   Love for the loveless ones tomorrow,
   Love for all the lovers too.

On the morrow is the day when Heaven and Earth first
   learned to mate;
when the Father from the clouds of Spring begot the
   Year's estate;

when the bridegroom-rain flowed down to slake the body
  of the bride,
feeding hungry offspring with its power, spread richly
  far and wide;
when blood of curving Heaven dripped to fill with life
  the foaming Main—
beautifully then Dione rose from out the nuptial rain,
Queen amid the two-legg'd watersteeds, the herds of
  crystal blue.

> *Love for the loveless ones tomorrow,*
> *Love for all the lovers too.*

Now Her breath has filled our blood and mind, it fills
  us through and through,
till in hidden ways each life obeys Her procreative will.
Through heaven and earth and sea beneath She passed
  and passes still:
strongly Her insinuating warmth through pathways of
  the seed
She has sent and taught the ways of birth and bade the
  world take heed.

> *Love for the loveless ones tomorrow,*
> *Love for all the lovers too.*

Trojan with the Latin stock She long past grafted, and
  She drew
once a maid of the Laurentians to mingle with her Son.
Mars obtained from Her the cloistered main, a shyly
  virgin nun;
straightway at Her hymeneal word that Sabine rape was
  done,
that the Roman race as citizens might worthily combine,
getting thus the race of Romulus and Caesar of Her line.

> *Love for the loveless ones tomorrow,*
> *Love for all the lovers too.*

Joy is still the fertilizing power, the fields know Venus near.

Love, Her child, is country born: so runs the certain tale we hear.

When the Earth in birth split open, up She took him to Her breast,

and with dainty kisses of the flowers She fed him and caressed.

> *Love for the loveless ones tomorrow,*
> *Love for all the lovers too.*

Deeply bedded, look, the bulls in broom with massive flanks now lie.

Every safety threading life must surely hail the marriage-tie.

Bleating through the shadows, look, among the hes the bitches throng.

Venus comes to tell the birds to be no niggards of their song.

Raucous-crying swans go winging by and crash across the pool,

and the nightingale is singing out where polar-shades are cool.

Surely it's a lover singing, one who sings a lover's joy,

not a wand'ring sufferer who laments her sister and her boy.

Loud she sings her heart out. I am mute. O when will my Spring come?

when the swallow's voice will be my voice, and I no longer dumb.

Lost the Muse, and now Apollo I no more may call my friend.

Thus by silence fell Amyclae, and that silence was her end.

63

Love for the loveless ones tomorrow,
Love for all the lovers too.

[*The* Vigil *seems composed for a spring-rite: see Pater's*
Marius the Epicurean. *But maybe for the pagan revival
of the fourth century. It makes a strong effort to univer-
salize Venus as the source of all earthly love and life; and
has an official touch in the stress on Venus as the ancestor
of Julius Caesar and the patroness of the Romans.
Dione is Venus. There is reference to the myth that she
was born of the castrated genitals of Kronos (Saturn)
falling into the sea. The Delian Maid is the huntress
Artemis (Diana). The God of Poets is Apollo. Note the
sudden romantic turn into loneliness at the end. The
luscious style in general shows the breakdown of classical
attitudes.*]

24. YOUR MISTRESS

Lucilius

O when she's all alone with you
and no one there to see,
she doesn't care how shabby she looks,
as shabby as can be.

But when another man turns up,
a different tune she sings,
she dons her ribbons, her robe and her fillets,
all of her finest things.

25. THE MATRON OF EPHESUS

Petronius

ONCE upon a time there lived in Ephesus a married woman of such shuddering virtue that females used to come in even from the countries roundabout to have a peep at her. So, when she buried her husband, she wasn't contented with doing the usual thing – following the bier with her hair flying wild and thumping her naked bosom in front of an admiring crowd. She followed the dead man right into his last resting-place and proceeded to weep and watch over the corpse day and night. All this was in an underground vault, the sort the Greeks use. It was no use her parents or other relations trying to stop her. She went on torturing herself and trying to starve to death. The officials were snubbed and left her to it. Everyone gave her up for dead and grieved for such a unique character among women.

So there she was, passing her fifth day of fast. As she grew weaker, a devoted maid sat by her side, weeping tear for tear with her and filling up the lamp set on the tomb whenever the flame showed signs of subsiding. In the city she was the only subject of conversation, and every single person of every class admitted that she shone forth as the one true model of chastity and love.

Now at this moment the governor of the province gave orders for some robbers to be crucified near the small structure in which the lady was lamenting her recent loss. So, next day, the soldier, on guard by the crosses to stop anyone from taking down a body for burial,

noticed a light glimmering quite distinctly among the
tombs, and heard the moans of a mourner. With a weak-
ness inherent in human nature, he was eager to find out
who groaned and what was going on.

So he went down into the vault. When he came into
view of a beautiful woman, he first halted in confusion,
as if he'd seen some prodigy, a spirit from the world
below. Then he saw the corpse lying there and watched
the woman's tears and the scratches of nails across her
face. He realized what the scene meant and that the
woman had found her loss too great to bear. So he
brought his supper down into the tomb and began
urging the mourner not to persevere in her unavailing
sorrow, not to break her heart with sobs that helped
nobody. For all men came to the same end and found
the same lasting home, and so on — all the string of
platitudes guaranteed to restore lacerated spirits to
equanimity.

But she ignored his attempts at sympathy and merely
tore her bosom more vehemently or pulled out hanks
of her hair and strewed them on the corpse. The soldier,
however, refused to be rebuffed. He went on trying to
encourage the woman and induce her to eat. At length
the maid, no doubt seduced by the smell of the wine,
stretched out her hand at his good-natured invitation;
and then, revived by the wine and the food, she seconded
him in the attack on her mistress's obstinacy.

'What good will it do you if you faint away with
hunger, if you bury yourself alive, if you resign your
breath before the fates demand it?

Think you that ashes or the buried man
can feel?

Why don't you start living all over again. Why don't

66

you shake off all this woman's folly and enjoy the comforts of daylight while you've still got the chance? The body of your husband lying there is the very thing that ought to be telling you: Live, live!'

People find it hard not to listen when they're being coaxed to eat something and stay alive. So the lady, famished after her several days' feast, allowed her resolve to be undermined. She filled herself up with food as greedily as the maid, who'd been the first to succumb.

Well, you know to what temptation mortal flesh is most exposed after a good meal. The soldier once more used the insinuating arguments that had won the lady into agreeing to live, but this time to break down her chastity. There he was, even in her modest eye, a young man not at all deficient in good looks, and with the gift of the gab. And at the same time the maid was advising her to listen to her kind heart and concluding with a quotation:

'Will you fight even with love you find delightful? and not recall in whose lands now you rest?'

No need to prolong the tale. The woman proved no more abstinent in one part of her body than in the other, and the conquering soldier had his way. They spent together not only the night when she thus embraced him but the next night as well, and the night after that, taking the obvious precaution of bolting the entry to the vault, so that any friend or stranger who came on a visit would imagine that the paragon of virtue had breathed her last over her husband's corpse.

The soldier, fascinated by the woman's beauty and his secret, bought all the delicacies his pay permitted, and conveyed them to the tomb the moment darkness fell. So the parents of one of the crucified men, noting how careless was the guard, took the body down one night and performed the necessary last rites over it.

In his absence from duty the soldier was thus circumvented; and next day, finding one of the crosses without its corpse, he was scared at the prospect of punishment and hurried to tell the lady what had happened. He told her that he wouldn't wait for a court-martial but would punish his negligence with his own sword. So she had better prepare a place for a second dead man and let the one vault of death immure both husband and lover.

The lady, however, was as compassionate as she was virtuous. 'The gods forbid,' she replied, 'that I should attend at one and the same time the funerals of the two men whom I love most dearly. I'd rather see a dead man crucified than a living man dead.'

She thereupon bade him remove her husband's corpse from the coffin and fix it up on the empty cross. The soldier took advantage of the provident woman's ingenious suggestion; and the people wondered next day by what means a dead man had ascended the cross.

26. EPIGRAMS

Martial

Bassa, we continually hear from you
that you are beautiful, and a virgin too.
But, Bassa, we begin to doubt it
when a girl has got so much to say about it.

*　　　*　　　*

Lesbia, you think a man should be
prepared for action instantly;
but bows aren't strung at every time and place.
However strongly you may press
with coaxing whisper and caress,
you spoil the whole thing when I see your face.

*　　　*　　　*

Afer goes always late to bed,
and can you wonder why?
Look at the woman he has wed,
with whom he has to lie.

*　　　*　　　*

Now Paula wants to marry me.
Too old, she makes me ill.
Yet I'd agree to marry her
if she were older still.

*　　　*　　　*

O, I'm the poet of world-wide fame.
My books all round you'll see.

My unmalicious jokes are quoted –
but why this jealousy?
There's many a racehorse I could name
who's better known than me.

* * *

Now, you'll admit, a better-matched couple
on this earth there couldn't be.
A very bad wife and a very bad husband –
I wonder you disagree.

* * *

You're the loveliest woman ever born,
also the most embraced.
Then be a shade less beautiful, please,
or learn to be more chaste.

* * *

Lydia's as broadly and capaciously developed
as the rump of a bronze equestrian statue
as a hoop going round with tinkly bells
as a wheel knockt by an acrobat from the springboard
as a worn-out shoe soaked with muddy water
as a widemeshed net spread open for wandering fieldfares
as an awning that doesn't belly in the wind in Poempey's
    Theatre
as a bracelet that's slipt from a consumptive prettyboy's
    arm
as a pillow widowed of its Leuconian stuffing
as ancient breeches of a poverty-stricken Briton
as a Ravenna pelican's filthy pouch.

The tale goes that I had this woman in a fishpond of the
    sea.
Myself, I think I had the fishpond.

27. PROVINCIAL OFFICIAL ON TOUR

Cicero

On the Hellespont is a town called Lampsacus, which stands among the first towns of the Province of Asia for renown and magnificence. The inhabitants are particularly friendly to all Roman citizens and are extremely peaceable and orderly people, outdoing almost all other Greeks in their preference of a quiet life above brawls and tumult. Now Verres pulled strings till he was sent on a mission to the King of Bithynia – a job he wanted for profit rather than patriotism. And in the course of his journey he turned up at Lampsacus, to the misfortune and problematic future of the place. For lodgings he was taken to the house of one Ianitor, while his staff were billeted on other hosts. According to his custom, in which his procedure was prompted by his passions, he at once laid on his staff (a set of dirty dogs, if there were any such) the commission of sniffing out and tracking down any maid or wife available, who would make it worth his while to stay on awhile in the town.

Among his company was one Rubrius, the very chap for such a post of pander, who at every stop exercised remarkable skill in ferreting out information. He now trotted up with the following news. A man named Philodamus, easily in birth, rank and property the first Lampsacene, had a daughter who was still unmarried and resided with her father – a creature of outstanding beauty, rumoured as well to be surprisingly virtuous and chaste. Verres, on hearing the story, was stirred up with a vehement desire for someone whom he had not only not seen with his own eyes but whom he merely heard about from a man speaking at second-hand. He announced that he would move his quarters immediately to Philodamus' house.

Ianitor, his host, who had no idea what was going on, feared that he had somehow given offence, and did his best to prevent the removal. So Verres, unable to think up any pretext for a change of lodgings, had to devise some other plan for his lewd intentions. He declared that Rubrius, his best of friends, his assistant in all his darkest doings, his confidant, was uncomfortably lodged; and he gave orders for his removal to the house of Philodamus.

When the latter was told, though unaware of the calamity being brewed for his family, he approached Verres and pointed out that a man of his standing shouldn't be burdened with such charges. When his turn came to receive a guest, he was used to put up governors and the like, not the mere attendants of a legate. But Verres, now furious against more obstructions to his lust, waved aside all these requests and explanations and gave orders for Rubrius to be introduced by force into the home of a man who was within his rights in closing the door.

However, Philodamus, seeing that he could not obtain his due respect, studied at least to preserve his courtesy and affability. Reputed to show always the utmost hospitality towards our people, he did not like to seem grudging in his reception of even such a nonentity as Rubrius. He arranged a tiptop dinner, being one of the richest townsmen, and asked Rubrius to invite anyone he liked, leaving only one place unfilled – that of the master of the house. He even sent out his son, an excellent young man, to dine with a relation.

Rubrius invited the whole staff to a man. Verres primed them with complete instructions as to their behaviour. They turned up early and lounged on the couches. Chit-chat was bandied about and the invitation given to drink in the Greek manner. The host encouraged them. They called for bigger winecups. Amid babble and enjoyment on all sides the banquet went on. Then Rubrius decided that the iron was sufficiently heated, and broke out, 'Hey there, Philodamus, why don't you call that daughter of yours to come in and join us?'

Philodamus, a man of much dignity and of ripe old age, was amazed at the rapscallion's demand. But, as he had to reply something, he remarked that it was not the custom of the Greeks to have women reclining with men at dinner-parties.

At once someone shouted across the room, 'Ho, we can't stand for an answer like that. Call the wench in.'

Rubrius at the same moment bade his slaves close the doors and themselves guard the threshold. Philodamus, realizing that the whole thing had been staged as a preliminary to carrying his daughter off by force, shouted for the servants, commanded them to leave him and think only of the girl's safety. And he sent one of them off to inform his son of the calamity descending on the house.

Meanwhile, the place was in an uproar. The slaves of Rubrius and those of the host were scrimmaging; and Philodamus, that respected citizen, was mobbed in his own home. Every man fought to save his own skin; and at last Philodamus was drenched in boiling water by Rubrius.

The son, on hearing what was afoot, rushed back to the house in a flurry of fear to succour his father's life and his sister's chastity. The whole town was thrown into

73

as great a rage on hearing of the enormity practised against such a man as Philodamus, and flocked in the darkness about the house. At this point Cornelius, Verres' lictor, who had been posted by Verres with his attendants (to convoy the ravished woman), was knocked on the head and killed. Some of the slaves were wounded. Rubrius himself was injured in the confusion; and Verres, seeing the commotion that his lust had conjured up, looked round for some way of escape.

Next day the citizens called an early assembly and debated what was the best course. Man after man harangued the crowd and carried weight according to his reputation; but not one man stood up who did not directly declare: 'There could be no fear, if we Lampsacenes avenged by answering violence the crime of Verres, that the Senate and people of Rome would feel it necessary to chastise our city. If the Roman legates were to establish as a law that no children of the folk in allied and foreign nations were to be secure from their lust, then it'd be better to suffer any fate than submit to such harrowing criminality.'

All agreed. Each man spoke in this vein according to the promptings of his heart. Then the whole assembly moved towards Verres' lodgings. They banged on the door with stones, hacked at it with swords, surrounded the walls with wood and faggots, and set fire to them. But the Roman citizens who were resident traders in the town came hurrying up. They begged the men to think less of the villainy shown by the legate and more of the respect due to his legation. They admitted the fellow's wickedness, but urged that he had failed in his schemes and would soon be gone, so that the Lampsacenes would do less wrong in sparing a scoundrel than in slaughtering a legate. So the wretch, even more a reprobate than Hadrian, had better luck. (For Hadrian, rousing Roman citizens beyond all tolerance by his usury, was burnt alive in his house at Utica; and his death was so well deserved that everyone laughed and no arrests were made.)

But as for Verres, scorched by the kindled flames yet escaping from his predicament, he was quite unable then or at any time to imagine what one earth he had done or what could have happened to cause such a fuss and bother.

[*From the Speeches against Verres for corruption as a governor.*]

28. WHO'S THE GIRL?

Catullus

Dear Flavius, it's a hopeless slut
some drab uncouth with careless hair,
or you'd not keep your mouth so shut:
some fever-stricken what's-its-name,
a tart, and you can't speak for shame.

But though you're mum, your sheets declare
that not alone your nights are spent,
the garlands and the Syrian scents,
the dints, the prints, the telltale creaks,
the obviously collusive bed.

Yes, everything about you speaks
except yourself, who shake your head.

But why? Your fagged distracted ways
can only mean a lecher's daze;
and so, whatever's right or wrong,
speak up. I merely want to raise
you and your love heaven-high in song.

29. THE GENERAL IS DRUNK

M. Caelius Rufus

THEY chafe the man as he lies sprawling in a tipsy lethargy, racking his whole frame with deep snores. His only response is to double his vinous belches. His celebrated lady-messmates are there, stretched sideways across the couches or else heaped promiscuously about. But they are wide-awake, stricken with terror. They see the enemy closing in upon them. They do their best to arouse the incapable general. They scream out his name. They futilely drap him about their shoulders. One of them coaxingly mumbles into his ear, another keeps on furiously striking him.

He recognizes the voice and touch of each woman and seeks to pull the nearest one down with an arm round her neck. He is too excited to sleep and too drunk to stay awake, and in a drowsy stupor he is carried out, tossed between the hands of centurions and harlots.

[*All that remains of the speech by which Caelius made his name, arraigning a general and using a new realism in his style.*]

30. WHERE ARE YOU, FRIEND?

Catullus

Excuse me if I anger you,
but where's your lurkhole in the dark?
I sought you in the Smaller Park,
the Circus and the Bookstalls too.
From Jove's great Temple in despair
to Pompey's Portico I ran
and stopped each wench who sidled there
with smiles to welcome-in a man.
'Bad girls,' I cried inquiringly,
'give up Camerius your prize.'
One spread her naked breasts for me,
'Between these tips of rose he lies.'

You'd have defeated Hercules.
Though I were brass like him of Crete
or Pegasus who skims the seas
or Perseus, wings upon his feet,
or Rhesus' mares with flanks of snow,
with all the wings of birds and gods
and all the might of winds that blow,
Camerius, I'd take the odds
that, broken in the zigzag race,
I'd faint away before the end
and fail to find your hiding-place.

Then must you still deny your friend?
Please give me some address or clue.
Be brave and tell me where you live.

Are girls of milk detaining you?
Lovers so tightly secretive
throw love's best fruits away, you'll find.
For Venus likes the ones who tell.
But keep your riddles. I don't mind
if in your love I share as well.

[*Written in 55 B.C. when Pompey's Portico was opened.*]

31. MARC ANTONY WOOS HIS OWN WIFE

Cicero

HE reached Saxa Rubra at four o'clock in the afternoon. There he took refuge in a certain low tavern, shut himself up, and drank hard till dusk. Then, driving full-speed to Rome in a cab, he arrived at his own house with his face all muffled up. The doorkeeper asked, 'Who are you?'

'A letter-carrier from the master.'

He was at once taken to the woman for whose sake he had come. He handed her the letter. She took it and read it with tears. For it was a lover's letter and the contents amounted to this: Never more would he have anything to do with that Actress, he had cast aside all the love he had had for her and transferred it back to the woman he addressed.

But when she went on weeping even more effusively, the tender-hearted man could bear it no longer. He unmuffled his face and threw himself on her neck. O, you good-for-nothing hooligan. That's the only phrase I can find to describe you. Was it to surprise your wife by turning up all of a sudden in this amorous masquerade that you struck Rome with terror by night and filled all Italy with alarm for many days?

[*From his Speeches attacking Antony and referring to the days of confused civil war after the murder of Caesar. The Actress was Cytheris: see next item.*]

32. ACTRESS AT A DINNER-PARTY

Cicero

I t's three o'clock and I've just lain down at table where I'm making a scribbled copy of this letter to you in my notebook.

'Where?' you'll ask.

At the house of Volumnius Eutrapelus. On the upper side lies Atticus and on the lower Verrius, both good friends of yours. Are you surprised then that we can take our servitude so cheerfully? What then am I to do? I ask you as a student of philosophy. Shall I moan? Shall I torture myself? What's the use of all that? And then again, for how long?

You'll say, 'Live in your books.'

Do you suppose that isn't exactly what I do? Could I live at all if I didn't? But even with my books there's a question not of growing weary but of having to stop sometime. When I leave then, although I'm not in the least a fusspot about menus – the one theme of inquiry you set the philosopher Dion – still I can't find any better way of putting in the hours before I take myself to bed.

Now listen to the rest of the story. Next below Eutrapelus has reclined Cytheris. At such a dinner-party, you cry, was found the great Cicero:

> *He who was noticed with surprise,*
> *he on whose face the Greeks all turned their eyes.*

But on my oath I never suspected she'd be here. However, even Aristippus, the Socratic philosopher, didn't blush when his copulations with Lais were thrown in his face.

'I have her,' he said, 'she doesn't have me.'

The joke goes better in the Greek. Find your own translation if you like. But that kind of thing left me cold as a young man, let alone now I'm ageing. I delight in a dinner-party. I have something to say on every subject that crops up (as the saying goes), and I soon change a groaning yawn into a bellow of delight.

[*Probably dated November 46* B.C. *For Cytheris, see previous item. A respectable woman sat at dinner, did not lie down like the men.*]

33. SUDDEN LOVE

Horace

The cruel mother of the Cupid-mob,
the son of Semele, and lewd Delight
have roused my heart once more to throb
and woken dreams I thought had taken flight.

At Glycera I gave a glance.
The girl's more milky-bright than Parian stone.
I love her pretty petulance,
no face so smoothly dazzling have I known.

Venus, full-length, has filled my veins,
deserting Cyprus. Now I'm not to sing
of Parthians scattering on the plains,
or Scythians, or any alien thing.

A living square of turf I need.
Bring vervain, lads, and incense, hurriedly.
Pour out old wine. A lamb must bleed,
a lamb must slake her thirst and ransom me.

[*Son of Semele; Bacchus, god of wine.*]

34. HOW A WOMAN SHOULD BEHAVE WHEN DINING WITH BOTH HUSBAND AND LOVER

Ovid

YOUR husband has been invited to the same dinner-party as we have. I only hope the food chokes him and he's carried out stiff. Am I to be a mere guest, with only the right to look at the body I love? And is someone else there to have the pleasure of touching you? Will you lean snuggling back with your head keeping warm the bosom of a wretch in the place below you – while he casually now and then rests his hand on your neck?

Who now will be surprised that a brawl broke out between the Lapiths and the Horsemen when a lovely woman was being married and the wine was put on the table? I don't live in a forest and my limbs are far from being those of a horse, but it's all I can do to keep my hands away from you. So get firmly into your head the etiquette for this dinner, and don't let the gales of the east blow my words out of that head of yours, nor the warm winds coming up from the south.

Try to come on ahead of your husband. Not that I've got the least idea what we can do if you arrive first. Still, slip along if you possibly can. When he stretches out on the couch, assume your best air of modest wifehood and go to join him, making sure you touch my foot without anyone noticing. Keep your eye on me and note every nod, every expression on my face. Catch the drift of my secret signs and make your answers. Without speaking, I'll tell you all sorts of things by my eyebrows, and you'll be able to read the words my meandering wine-wet fingers trace. When you remember how I've held you under me, press that pretty finger on your flowersoft cheeks. If there's something in my behaviour that you object to, give yourself a delicate nip on the lobe of the ear. And when I do or say anything that makes you ripple inside with pleasure, give the ring on your finger a twist and keep on twisting it.

Take hold of the table with your hand, just as people in prayer take hold of the altar, when you wish something nasty for your husband, who deserves the worst he gets. If you're the clever girl I think you are, tell your husband to drink the cup he's mixed for you; then in a low voice ask the servant for the wine you want. I'll promptly take up the cup you put down, and I'll drink just at the place where you touch it with your sipping lips. If he presses on you some morsels that he's tasted first, reject what his mouth has soiled. And don't let him pull you up close with his arms around your neck. And don't lie back with your gentle head on his nauseating chest. Don't give him a chance to catch at your breasts, your temptingly close nipples. And above all don't let him get at you with a kiss. If you're fool enough to kiss him, our love-affair will come out at once; for I'll shout out, 'You're mine, not his,' and I'll make a grab at you.

Still, those sort of fumblings at least I'll be able to spot. I'll be much more worried and suspicious about what is going on under your clothes. Don't touch his thigh with yours. Don't cross your leg over his. Don't let your dainty foot tickle his uncouth leg. To my misery, I'm tormented with all kinds of images, because there are so many wanton tricks I've been up to myself. It's fear of my own precedent that gets me down. Often beneath the cloth have my girl and I forestalled our hasty delights without anyone being the wiser. But I'm sure you'll never do such an office for him. All the same, keep the cloths away from all the parts where something might be happening. Keep on urging your husband to drink up, but don't mix kisses up with your cajoleries; and do your best to add more wine by stealth when he drinks. If only he is stretched out in a drunken doze, we'll see if we can't take the opportunity to establish contact. When you rise to go home, everyone else will rise too. Remember to walk home in the middle of the crowd. There we'll be able to find one another; and whatever part of me you can rub against, rub.

Alas, all this advice of mine can be of use anyway for a few hours at most. As we all say good-bye I'll have to let you go in. At night you are your husband's to lock and bolt in; and I with all my tears can follow you to the obdurate door, but no farther. Then he'll take all the kisses he wants, and more than kisses; and you'll have to give him openly what I get only with a deal of muffling stealth. But there's something you can do – you can surrender with the worst grace possible, with all the stiffening resistance you can manage. Don't whisper a single love-word and let the whole thing be bungled. I offer up my prayer that he gets nothing out of the sorry business; but if you can't spoil it for him, at least don't get any pleasure out of it yourself. And whatever happens when you get home, tell me tomorrow in the plainest and most explicit language that you didn't do the slightest thing to help him.

35. LYDIA BEWARE

Horace

When, Lydia, I have heard you praise
Telephus' smooth hard arms, his flushing neck,
I feel my liver in a blaze
and bile arises, difficult to check.

My colour comes and goes, my mind
wavers as well, and tears unheeded roll
across my cheeks, till you may find
what flames are harrowing my hidden soul.

I burn, if loosely drunken fights
have stained your gleaming shoulders in the dark,
or if the ardent boy of nights
has set on bitten lips the lover's mark.

Believe me. Vainly you expect
a constant love from one whose reckless force
can wound the lips that Venus decked
with sweetness from her purest nectar-source.

Thrice happy they, more happy still,
the loving hearts that never need to stray.
No quarrels break their wedded will,
they never part until the final day.

36. ALL THE GIRLS LOVE A SOLDIER

Plautus

Pyrgopolynices (to his orderlies, as he struts up and down, with his servant Artotrogus mimicking him from behind). Put some elbow-grease into it now, make that shield of mine shine properly, get the razzle-dazzle of the noon-sun into the metal, so that when I wave it I'll blind all the blinking enemy. *(Draws his sword.)* Look at this poor sword of mine; it needs a comforting word, clanking away at my side many a long day with complaints at being so idle, when all the while he's mad, poor lad, to be up and out and slashing all our foemen into mincemeat. *(Looks round.)* Now where on earth is that servant of mine?

Artotrogus. Here I am, sir, just where I ought to be, at the side of our bold hero whom nobody can beat, bless his noble looks. It's my opinion, sir, that Mars the god of war would think twice before putting himself on your level or trying his might against yours.

Pyrgo. (reminiscently). Who was that chap I got out of a tight corner at the Battle of Maggotsfield? You know, the commanding officer was old Bumboomwarsky Lord Chaffermuck, the grandson of Neptune.

Arto. O yes, I remember, sir. Of course, you mean that fellow in golden armour – you just took a deep breath and blew his army away, like I've seen the wind sweep leaves off, or a roof of thatch.

Pyrgo. That was nothing, anybody could have done that, really.

Arto. No, bejazes, though it was a mere bit of cake to

some of the things you've done that I could mention *(to the audience)* if I wanted to tell lies. Now if anyone of you knows a bigger fantasist, a more colossally bounding braggart, he can have him for his own with full legal rights. There's only one redeeming point about him: his olive-compote does make you smack your lips.

Pyrgo. (turning). Where have you got to?

Arto. (jumping behind him). Here I am, sir. But what about that elephant in India, now? I did like the way your fist simply cracked his forearm like a stick.

Pyrgo. What's that? the elephant's arm?

Arto. Leg I meant, sir, foreleg.

Pyrgo. O, I just gave him a casual tap.

Arto. Just so, sir. Why, if you'd really put yourself into the blow, you'd have clean transpliflicated the beast, sir, hide, flesh, bone and all the rest.

Pyrgo. Let's stop talking about these trifles.

Arto. Yes, sir, I agree, it really isn't worth while recounting all your dashing deeds to someone like me who knows all there is to know about you. *(To the audience, as his master goes on parading up and down.)* It's this stomach of mine that brings me into such misery. I've got to let his words go rasping in my ears or I won't have any of his food to go sliding down my throat. There's no whopper he can tell that I won't okay.

Pyrgo. Hmm now, what was it I was going to say?

Arto. I've got it, sir. I agree absolutely. I'll swear to every word of it. I recall you doing the whole thing.

Pyrgo. Doing what?

Arto. What? Let me think now. Whatever you did, of course.

Pyrgo. Look here, have you got about you—

Arto. Notebooks, sir, yes. That what you want? Here they are, pen too.

Pyrgo. You're pretty good at reading my mind.

Arto. It's up to me, sir. Study you like a book, learn all your ways, sir, and guess what you want before you've found the words for it. That's me, sir.

Pyrgo. (with assumed indifference). So you remember, eh?

Arto. Every little detail. *(Calculating on his fingers.)* A hundred and fifty in Cilcia . . . a hundred in that place, where is it? Scittle-brigandia, of course. Thirty Sardines, I mean Sardinians. Sixty Macs from Macedonia. That's the total list of the men you laid low in one day, sir. Signed all correct.

Pyrgo. But the complete list, the whole bloody lot?

Arto. Seven thousand, sir, exactly. To a nought.

Pyrgo. (meditating). Yes, it ought to come at least to that. Your arithmetic is remarkably good.

Arto. I haven't kept any written records, sir. I can trust my memory. Just nick the items up there.

Pyrgo. I congratulate you. Jolly good show.

Arto. It's the victuals what does it.

Pyrgo. As long as you show yourself as good a soldier as you've done so far, I give you my word that you'll never stop eating, not for a minute, and you shall share my rations with me.

Arto..(excited). What about that time in good old Cappadocia, sir, when you would have dealt with five hundred of the bastards with a single swipe, only I hadn't sharpened your sword proper that morning?

Pyrgo. Aw, well, they were only a lot of measly infantry – footsloggers – so I thought I might as well let the stinkers live.

Arto. Why should I mention it to you, sir? – something the whole wide goggling world knows – that you're the one and only Pyrgopolynices anywhere to be seen, standing all alone in knock-em-down deeds, a good looker and the world's champ? All the women are wriggling with love for you, sir, and who can blame 'em, when you're such a smasher in looks? Those pieces, for instance, who grabbed hold of me from behind by the cloak, only yesterday.

Pyrgo. (trying to seem unconcerned). What did they say to you by the way?

Arto. O, they just keep on asking things about you, sir. Is he that ancient hero Achilles? says one of 'em. No, no, I says, he's his brother. Goodness gracious, says the other one, that's why he's such a fine handsome gent. Did you get an eyeful of all that gorgeous hair he's got? Ooo, how lucky are the girls that jump into bed with him for a cuddle.

Pyrgo. (settling his cloak). So they really said all that, did they, the little hussies?

Arto. Why, didn't they beg me to lead you past their place today, just as if you are a whole parade?

Pyrgo. (yawning). It's really quite a bother to be afflicted with good looks.

Arto. I suppose it must be, sir. The women are a pest, aren't they, with the soppy way they come round, teasing and solicitating me, sir, yes absolutely exsopliflicating me to let 'em have just one little peep in at your charms. Why, they keep on sending me so many piffling messages I haven't any time to attend to you, sir.

Pyrgo. (with an effort). All the same, it's time for us to go to the Forum so I can pay the recruits I enlisted yesterday. King Seleucus you know entreated me most urgently to raise and enrol a regiment for him; and so I've made up my mind to devote this day to obliging His Majesty.

Arto. It's all the same to me, sir.

Pyrgo. (to his orderlies). Come along, scum. *(They go out, with Artotrogus lagging behind his master and making fun of his movements.)*

91

37. SOFTNESS IS BEST

Lucilius

No hard and beefy thing
like a fighter in the ring
may yet a woman stand.
But pliant are her charms
and gently soft her arms,
and still your open hand
may most agreeably rest
upon her milkfilled breast.

38. THE GIRL FROM TARENTUM

Naevius

She wanders like a shuttlecock,
       from side to side she flutters,
she makes a lover with a wink,
       with every word she utters.

She's welcomed by the younger folk,
       and flirtingly she stands,
then sits and rouses someone else,
       toes wriggling, squeezing hands.

She blows a kiss, she gazes round,
       she turns and shows her ring,
to one she tips the sign of love,
       with one she stops to sing.

39. FROM THE WALLS OF POMPEII

Anon. Scribblers

[i]

I'm dazed and weak, and sleep has fled away.
I'm burned with sweltering love by night and day.

[ii]

It's the Lover who writes, the Sod who reads, it's
    clear.
The Listener twitches and itches, and he who goes by
    is a Queer.
And me, I'm the Bear's-dinner, I'm the Twerp who
    stands reading here.

[iii]

Who forbids Love? who's the policeman of lovers?

[iv]

Do look and see what I'm suffering, Petrulla, I beg you.

[v]

Venerusa, I hope you may love him well.

[vi]

Figulus loves Idaia.

[vii]

Fortunatus you sweet little darling you great fornicator,
someone who knows you writes this.

[viii]

Modestus had a tryst here with Albana.

[ix]

G. Julius Promogenius was here on time, what's keeping you?

[x]

I'm going off, good-bye my Sava, keep on loving me.

[xi]

Eulalus, good luck to you and your wife Vera, may you both have a good time close together.

[xii]

O poppet I was sent to you by your lover
and now I see you and see that you are lovely.

[xiii]

I'd give the world to lovely wenches free.
But girls whom all can take are not for me.

[xiv]

Crescens, if someone lures my girl to meet him,
on far-off mountain-tops a bear will eat him.

[xv]

He binds the winds from blowing, who chides at lovers
and tries to stop the waters of springs from flowing.

[xvi]

The blonde makes me scorn all brunettes,
        she's so far set above them.
I'll turn them down if I can;
        if I can't, I'll reluctantly love them.

[xvii]

In vain this town for tender embraces you scan.
No girl awaits the love-notes of a man.

[xviii]

Let the lover flourish
            and let the unloving perish
But a double death if he uses his breath
            for reproving our loving.

[xix]

Farewell you splendid female snuggery.

[xx]

Jarinus had a girl here with Athetus.

[xxi]

Here I recall I had a girl of late.
The intimate details I shall not relate.

[xxii]

If anyone sits down here, let him read this announcement
first of all: if he wants to have a girl, look for Attice,
charge 16 coppers, a high-class girl.

[xxiii]

Prima was here with her Lover, Prima, Prima was here a
moment ago with Sparitundiolus.

[xxiv]

You've had eight jobs; now it only remains for you to
double the list and make it sixteen. You've been a pub-
waiter, you've made pottery, you've dealt in salted fish,
you've done bakery, you've been a farmer, you've made
small bronze oddments, you've been a street-hawker, now

you make little flasks. If only you'll hire yourself out to
the ladies, you'll have run the whole gamut.

[xxv]

May yours be the luck, Sabina, to blossom unfading,
your beauty unwithered. Long as a girl may you stay.

[xxvi]

May you perish, sweet love, for I love you so much that I
perish, Taine, my sweetest darling.

[xxvii]

Molis laments his loneliness.

[xxviii]

Vibius Restitutus slept here all on his own and longed for
his Urbana.

[xxix]

C. Valerius Venustus Soldier of the First Praetorian Co-
hort Company of Rufus, I had a night of most satisfactory
embraces in this bed.

[xxx]

Successus the Weaver loves Coponia's servant-girl.
Iris she's named. But she doesn't mind his sigh.
She doesn't. He keeps on pleading. She just pities him.
His rival Severus wrote this up. Good-bye.

[xxxi]

You who burst with jealousy you
take care though I don't want to prove what's true
who's handsomer, most worthy and fine chap of us two.

I said it, I wrote it. You love Iris and she doesn't mind
your sign at all. Severus to Successus, as I wrote it, that's
the way things are, Severus.

[*The last three consist of the exchanges between the two
lovers of Iris. Successus in his effort to rebut what
Severus says becomes wildly ungrammatical.*]

40. SETTLING THE ACCOUNT
AT AN INN

Anon.

'Landlady, let's have the bill.'
'You had a sextarius-worth of wine. Bread, one copper.
Porridge, two coppers.'
'That's correct.'
'A girl, èight coppers.'
'Yes, that's absolutely correct.'
'Hay for your mule, two coppers.'
'That mule will be the ruin of me.'
[*From the wall of a tavern at Aesernia.*]

41. APPLES

Petronius

You send me golden apples, Martia dear.
You send me fruit of the shaggy chestnut too.
Thanks for your apples, thanks, my lovely girl,
thanks for your nuts. But what I want is you.

Come if you will with apples sour to taste.
Your touch will make the honey-tinctures fall.
But if you say you're stopped from coming, kiss
the apples first and I'll devour them all.

98

42. A SLAVE-GIRL CAN BE TOO PRETTY

Plautus

'She'd cause a scandal, her features are far too
        bewitching,
if she strolled with a lady abroad. The people would
        pour
staring and leering, winking and whistling and
        twitching,
calling, molesting, serenading her door.
The charcoal marks of her praise on my door they'd
        scrawl;
and nowadays at no malice or lies they blench.
So my wife and myself immediately they'd call
a pair of panders preying upon the wench.'

'What then? I agree you've recounted the way they'd
        behave.'

'I'll buy my mother a bulky podge of a slave,
not a bad worker, but graced with a puddeny face,
right enough for a housewife, Egyptian or Syrian born,
who'll spin and bear lashes if need be, and grind the
        corn.'

43. MODEST GIRLS

Aulus Gellius

PLUTARCH in the first book of his work on the Soul discusses disorders that affect our minds, and records that at one time practically all the maidens of the town of Miletus were suddenly and for no apparent reason carried away by the desire to die. So they began hanging themselves in droves. When this went on day after day, and no remedy of the doctors had the least effect on their resolve, the Milesians passed a decree that all girls who committed suicide by hanging should be borne to the grave stark-naked, along with the rope they used to destroy themselves. At once, put off by the shame of such an immodest burial, the girls stopped doing away with themselves.

44. MY SORT OF GIRL

Ausonius

Here's the mistress that I choose.
Careless brawls she won't refuse
and bawdy words she'll often use.
Lovely, lively, loose in act,
she'll smack and let herself be smacked,
and smacked will snuggle to a kiss.
But if she's not at all like this
and lives a chastely straightened life—
I tremble. She will be my wife.

45. PRIMIGENIA FLIRTS

Written on Pompeian Walls:

1. By the Roman Gate at Nuceria you may seek out Novellia Primigenia, in Venus Street.
2. Sabinus was here with Primigenia.
3. Primigenia, Primigenia, good-bye.
4. How happy we are to have known Primigenia.
5. Good-bye Primigenia keep well.
6. Welcome to Primigenia the sweetest and most darling of all girls in the world, our best wishes.
7. Cornelius sends the biggest possible bundle of good wishes to Primigenia.
8. Secundus with Primigenia meet here.

On a Tomb along the Road to Herculaneum and Naples:

9. Good wishes to Primigenia of Nuceria.

And in a tavern at Herculaneum, the following record of a night-out, with a note about the girl on the same wall:

10. Apelles, chamber-valet of Caesar, dined here in the most delightful way with Dexter and they each had a girl together. Apelles and his brother Dexter charmingly had a girl here twice a double. Two comrades were here and when the hopeless waiter took too long over everything – his name was Epaphroditus – they didn't lose much time in kicking him out of doors; they spent most agreeably (including the girls) $105\frac{1}{2}$ sesterces.

Each paid 14, bread 3, fried specialities (three) 12, scents (four) 12 – 51 sesterces the dinner, 54½ the girls.

Hermeros wishes all the best to Mistress Primigenia, come to Puteoli and in the Timinian Street at the place of the banker Messius ask for Hermeros freedman of Phoebus.

46. IN LOVE WITH TWO GIRLS AT ONCE

Ovid

You used to tell me, Graecinus –
yes, you were the one, I am sure, I remember
       each word –
that a man may love two girls at the same time.
You tricked me into it.
It's all your fault I was caught unarmed and
       napping.
Look, to my shame, I'm mad about
two girls at the same moment.

Both are delightful.
Both spend much time and trouble on their
       clothes,
and which knows more than the other is hard
       to say.
The first's more beautiful than the second,
the second's more beautiful than the first.
The first pleases me more than the second,
the second pleases me more than the first.
My passions eddy to and fro.
I'm like a skiff sent helterskelter by a changeable
       wind.

I'm most distracted.
Why, Venus, keep on doubling my despairs?
wasn't one piece enough to break my heart?
why go on sticking leaves upon the trees,
stars in the crowded heavens, and waterdrops
in the enormous ocean?

Still, better too much love
than desolation with no love at all.
I wish my enemies a dull and serious life.
I wish my enemies a solitary bed
in which they toss in stiff and restless poses.
Myself, I want for ever cruel Love
to prick me out of sluggish slumbers.
I want my bed to creak with more
than loneliness. I want my girl,
unhindered in her naughtiness,
to make me die and die again.
And if one girl can't do the job,
let two of them proceed to kill me.

I'm not at all a hefty chap.
but I've my vigours all the same.
It's fat, not sinews, that I lack.
And joy renews my flanks for joy.
I've never let a woman down.
And often, busy through the long delicious night,
I've shown myself a stalwart in the morning.
Happy the man, I say,
who proves the full delights of love.
I pray the gods to let them be the cause
of my ecstatic end.

47. THE FULLER'S WIFE

Apuleius

THE wife of my old pal the fuller always seemed a woman of the choicest morals, and folk said that she ruled the roost in her husband's house most virtuously; but she burst out at last in a muffled love-affair with a young fellow. Now, as they met as often as they could squeeze in an unsuspected embrace, it came about that once when the fuller and I returned from the Baths to supper there were the two of them fast-hugging.

Startled by our premature arrival, the woman could improvise no better method of concealment than to push her lover under a high wicker-cage draped round with clothes that were being exposed to the bleaching fumes of sulphur. Thinking that he was snugly hidden, she sat blithely down to share the supper with us. All this while, however, the young man was drawn to inhale the suffocating clouds of acrid vapour given off by the burning sulphur that surrounded him; and (the usual effect of that lively sublimate) he could not resist repeatedly sneezing. The husband who sat facing his wife heard this sound come from behind her, and thought it was her product. So he exclaimed, 'Lord save you,' as is usual in such circumstances.

Then came a second sneeze, a third sneeze, and a whole volley of sneezes – till, at last, astonished at this excessive sternutation, he began to realize the facts of the case. Pushing back the table, he knocked the cage over and revealed the man panting for breath and almost strangulated. Furiously indignant at this outrage, he roared for his sword and would have cut the throat of the swooning fellow had I not with a struggle restrained him from a deed which would have brought the law down upon us all. I asseverated that his injurer would soon perish from convulsions without involving us in any guilt. Softened not so much by my argument as by sheer necessity, he dragged the choking young man into the next alleyway. While he was doing this, I pressed his wife and at last persuaded her to leave the shop for a while and shelter herself with friends until time had cooled her husband's hot blood. For I had no doubt that in his choleric fit he would do himself and his wife some unfortunate damage. Anyhow, by this time I had sampled more than enough of my friend's, and so I decided to go home.

48. TELL ME HER NAME

Horace

To brawl with winecups born for pleasantness
is Thracian. Take the barbarous trick away.
   Bacchus prefers to smile and bless.
     Hey, stop this bloody fray.

A Median dirk looks bad amid our joys
of wine and lamplight. Why, you're all possessed.
   Come, fellows, cease this wicked noise,
     down on your elbows rest.

You bid me try the strong Falernian?
First let Megulla's brother tell us why
   he looks a happy stricken man—
     whose arrow bids him die?

What, you won't speak? Then I shan't drink in turn,
and yet I'll swear the girl you find a lure
   won't make you blush although you burn,
     some decent wench I'm sure

and gently made. So please confide your sin.
My ears are safe. Good heavens, so that's your friend!
   What a Charybdis sucks you in—
     you're worth a better end.

No witch, no wizard with his poison-brew,
no god could save the man whom she embroils.

No Pegasus could drag him through
the monster's triple coils.

[*Charybdis, woman-monster of the whirlpool; Pegasus, winged horse, whom Bellerophon rode in slaying the triple monster, the Chimaera.*]

49. GIRL INTO BOY

The Elder Pliny

WE find in the Annals that in the consulship of
Q. Licinius Crassus and G. Cassius Longinus (171 B.C.)
a girl at Casinum was changed into a boy in the house of
her parents and on the instructions of the diviners was
deported to a desert island. Licinius Mucianus has put
on record that he saw at Argos one Arescontes, whose
name had been Arescusa; that she had even been
married as a wife, but after a while grew a beard, became a man, and took a wife of her own; and that at
Smyrna also he had seen a boy who underwent the same
sort of change. I myself, in Africa, saw L. Cossutius, a
citizen of Thysdrus, who had been changed suddenly
from a woman into a man in the middle of the marriage
rites. He is still alive as I write.

There are also persons who from birth are bisexual,
whom we term hermaphrodites. They were formerly
called androgynes and regarded as frightening prodigies
but now are instruments of pleasure.

50. PRAYER TO THE GARDEN GOD

Anon.

Listen, Priapus, while I pray.
A painted wench is mocking me.
She won't consent nor yet refuse
but still finds reasons to delay.
O teach me some successful ruse.
The daintiest flowers then I'll choose
and crown your godhead gratefully.

51. CAUGHT OUT

Ovid

[*Ovid writes indignantly to repel the charge that he has seduced his mistress's servant-girl. Then he chats with the girl herself.*]

Look here, are you never going to be tired of making up fresh charges and accusations? Though I can always prove that you've got things wrong and misjudged me, I get bored with having to go again and again into the same sort of argument. If I happen to glance up at the top row in the marble theatre, you pick out some woman from the mob there and insist on being upset by her. If some pretty girl chances to look my way without the slightest expression on her face, you are at once suspicious that something's hidden under her lack of interest. If I drop a word of praise about some girl, you have to be hauled away from getting at her luckless locks with your nails. If I find faults in a girl, then I'm covering up my attraction. If I happen to be in boisterous health, I'm accused of being indifferent towards you. If I'm off colour, then I'm dying of love for someone else.

I only wish I was conscious of having done something wrong; for if a man deserves what he gets, he endures his punishment with equanimity. But it's come about that you accuse me without any cause at all. You're so ready to believe anything you hear at random, you ensure that I can't take your anger in the least seriously. Just notice how the long-eared ass in his wretched lot shambles leisurely along, taking no notice of the endless blows that tyrannize over him.

And now you've thought up something new. Cypassis, that excellent toilet maid of yours, is blamed for having supplanted her mistress. I only pray the gods to take better care of me: if I should feel any inclination to a lapse, I trust I'll do better than a gutter-born wench of a downtrodden class. What free man would want to tangle with a slave and embrace a whip-mangled body? Not to mention that she is highly skilled at doing your hair, a valuable servant with well-trained hands. Can you imagine that I'd do such a thing with a servant who's faithful to you? Ask yourself why. Only that I might earn a snub to cap my letting you down? I swear by Venus and by the Bow of the Winged Boy that I am accused of a crime I have never committed.

*　　*　　*

Cypassis, you know how to do a lady's hair in a thousand different ways, but you're so good at it that you should have only goddesses as your clients. I have found you out in our delightful little affair to be no novice in love. You're useful indeed to your mistress, but even more serviceable to me. Who, I wonder, blabbed about our stolen caresses? How on earth did Corinna hear about your escapade? Is it my fault? did I blush? did I make a slip in some expression and give a guilty sign of our clandestine amours? I, who have declared roundly that any man who pulls a slave girl into his bed must be of unsound mind?

The hero Achilles was inflamed by the beauties of the looted daughter of Brises. Cassandra the slave-priestess of Phoebus was beloved by the Field Marshal of the Greek army. I am no greater a man than either of those big noises: why then should I consider it a disgrace to do what the kings and the conquerors took in their stride?

But when she fixed her angry eyes upon you, I saw a blush spreading all over your cheeks. But as for me, you'll remember the quicker presence of mind I showed in taking an oath on the great Godhead of Venus. Ah, goddess, be kind to me and instruct the warm south wind to bear away over the ocean the perjuries of an unsullied mind. And you, Cypassis, give me the sweet reward of your company for today. Why refuse me, you ungrateful girl? Why keep on inventing new reasons for being scared? It's enough to have laid one of your superiors under an obligation. But if in your folly you turn me down now, I'll inform against you with full details of what happened last time. I myself will be the betrayer of my betrayal. I'll tell Corinna all the spots in which I've met you, how often we met, and how many times we did the deed, and just what the deed was.

52. TO CHLORIS GROWING OLD

Horace

O clamp a stop upon the game,
wife of the penniless Ibycus. Desire
   no more this drudgery of shame.
Leave off – you're ripe now for the funeral pyre –

   thrusting among the girls at play
and spreading on their starry gleams a cloud.
   Your daughter Pholoe charms us, gay,
yes, Chloris, but not you. The girl's allowed

   to storm young fellows in their bed,
for she's a bacchant whom the timbrels craze.
   With Nothus now she hopes to wed
and like a wanton roe she skips and strays.

   O leave the wool Luceria grows
and leave the lute for other hands to hold,
   the burning blossom of the rose
and jars drained greedily to the dregs. You're old.

53. HARMLESS PRANK

Cicero

You say he raped an actress and allege that this event
occurred at Atina, when he was in early youth, by a sort
of customary licence towards theatrical folk, familiar

112

in the towns. Why, what a very well-behaved young
fellow he must have been if the only imputation against
him relates to a more or less harmless prank — and even
that didn't happen.

54. THE BARMAID

Anon.

O Syrian dancing-girl with the filleted hair,
who taught you to swing your flanks with that shiver and
  shake?
She's dancing drunk in the tavern's smoky air,
lewd wench, to the clicketing sound the castanets make.

Why stay in the dusty heat where everything withers?
Come here, lie down, and be drunk awhile, you fool.
Look, tankards, cups, bowls, roses, flutes and zithers,
and a trellis-arbour shadowed by reeds and cool.

In a cave full of music, like Pan's own cave, you can
  stretch,
the piping's the sort you hear in the open sky,
thin wine just drawn from a pitchy cask they'll fetch,
and, brabbling and murmuring, water goes swiftly by.

Look, there are wreaths from crocus and violets wrought,
gold melliot mixed with the rose's crimson hue.
From the virgin stream of Achelois are brought
lilies in willow baskets, and all for you.

Look, little cheeses drying in baskets of rush,

and plums that come to their sweetness in autumn
    weather;
chestnuts and apples with red that is pleasantly lush,
look, fine Ceres and Love and Bacchus together.

Look, reddened blackberries, grapes in placid clusters,
sea-green cucumbers hanging from tendrils of shade.
Look, the arbour-god – with his willow-hook he blusters,
but even his terrible middle won't make us afraid.

Hither, O wanderer. The little ass sweats and he faints,
the dear little ass is Vesta's own darling. So spare.
The crickets are splitting the thickets with shrilling
    complaints,
the lizard is lurking cool in a bramble-lair.

Be wise and drench out the heat with wine in a glass
or a crystal cup, if that's how you like your wine.
Lie tired in the vine-shade and let the summer hours
    pass
and round your nodding head let the roses entwine.

Yes, reap the kisses from someone mouth-open, kindly.
Death to the fellow who lifted his highbrow and frowned.
Why keep your wreaths for the ashes huddled blindly?
See your life and not your tombestone with roses
    crowned.

To hell with the future. Bring wine and the dice-box
    here.
'I'm coming, so kiss,' says Death, and pinches my ear.

55. THE CHARMING SERVANT-GIRL

Apuleius

'MY dearest Lucius,' said Byrrhaena, 'beware with might and main of the wicked arts and vicious seductions of this Pamphile who's married to your host Milo. She is a witch of the first rank and accounted mistress of every necromantic chant. By merely breathing on twigs and pebbles and suchlike ineffectual things she knows how to drown the whole light of the starry universe in the depths of hell, back in its ancient chaos. For as soon as she sees an attractive youth, she is on tenterhooks of admiration, and she rivets her eyes and her lustful mind upon him. She sows her blandishments, she invades his spirit, she snares him in unbreakable bonds of bottomless love. And those who do not comply at once, she loathes, and in a flash she whisks them into stones or cattle or any animal she chooses – or else she simply wipes them out. That is why I am alarmed for you, and consider that you ought to beware. For she inflames a man beyond redemption; and you, young and handsome as you are, are an apt victim.'

Thus Byrrhaena warned me, apprehensively enough, but she merely excited my interest. As soon as I heard her mention the Art of Magic, than which nothing was nearer to my heart's desire, than a strong compulsion made me yearn to attain the described mastery, though I should have to pay heavy fees for it, though I should fling myself with a running jump into the very abyss.

Trembling with distracted haste I extricated myself from Byrrhaena's grasp as if from shackles, blushed, and bidding her farewell dashed excitedly off to the house of my host Milo. And while I scurried along like a madman, I was saying to myself, 'Come now, Lucius, keep your wits about you and look alive-o. Here is the desired chance. Put out your hand and take the thing you've prayed for so long. Satiate your heart with Marvels. Discard all puerile fears. Grapple as if you meant business. But renounce all amorous connexion wheresoever with your hostess, and respect the nuptial sofa of the upright Milo. On the other hand sue and woo the servant-girl Fotis strenuously. For she is charmingly shaped, sportive in her ways, and decidedly talkative. Last evening, when you retired to rest, she conducted you obligingly into the bedroom, and laid you soothingly in bed, and rather lovingly drew up the bedclothes. And then her reluctant face showed how little she liked leaving only that one goodnight kiss upon your brow. And on the doorstep she turned her head, and smiled again, and could not go. Good luck and speed to your need, my lad; and come what may, a breach must be made through Fotis.'

Debating these matters, I reached Milo's front door and entered, with the question answered (as the saying goes) overwhelmingly in the affirmative. I did not, however, find Milo or his wife at home. My darling Fotis was alone in charge. She was preparing the stuffing for some black pudding and was mincing the pigs' tripes, some of which stood finely shredded on the sideboard, ready for mixing with a gravy that tickled my nostrils with its succulently wafted steam.

She was neatly clad in a linen apron, with a shining scarlet stomacher which gathered her dress up high under her meeting breasts; and she was stirring the stockpot with her rosy little hands moving round and round above it. And as she stirred and turned the meat, she herself stirred and vibrated congruously all over her supple body. Her loins softly undulated, and her agile spine swayed and rippled in time, as she placidly stirred the pot.

I was entranced by the sight, and stood in mute admiration. At last I addressed the girl. 'How finely, my dear Fotis, how gaily you stir your buttocks as you stand over the pot. What a honeyed relish I see you getting ready. A happy man, a blessed man, is he that you will let dip finger there.'

'Be off, you poor young fellow,' answered the young chatterbox, never at a loss for a repartee. 'Be off from my fireplace. Keep your distance. If the tiniest spark of that heat grazes you, you'll be scorched to the gizzard, and no one will be able to quench you but myself. For I'm very good at putting choice spice into pots or beds, and making them both equally appetizing.'

Chattering thus, she glanced at me and smiled; and I did not leave the room till I had diligently scrutinized every angle of her charm. But why divagate into detail. It has always been the prime concern of my life to observe in public the heads and tresses of beautiful women, and then to conjure up the image at home for leisurely enjoyment. This procedure is based on a clear and rationally determined proposition. Firstly, that Hair is the most important (visible) portion of the body, and that from its prominent position it first provokes attention. Secondly, that Hair by its natural hues provides that comeliness for the head which the gay tints of flowering dresses provide for the other limbs.

Moreover, most women, to commend their natural charms and graces, discard all mufflers, throw open their cloaks, and proudly delight in exhibiting their naked breasts, knowing that there is more delectation in the rosy gloss of the skin than in the golden sheen of a dress.

On the other hand (though even the supposition is irreligious and I pray that there may never be an instance of so horrible a monstrosity) if you despoil the most surprisingly beautiful woman of her hair, and denude her face of its natural accommodation – though she were dropped down from heaven, conceived of the seafoam, cradled among the waves, though she (I say) were Venus herself, though she were ringed round by the three Graces, and environed with the whole mob of Cupids, and laced with her love-girdle, fragrant as cinnamon and dewy with balsamum – yet if she came out bald, she would not be able to seduce even her own husband.

What satisfying hues and tangled lustres burn in woman's Hair. Sometimes it briskly repels the flash of the sun; sometimes it is absorbed into a softer penumbra or glistens with varying toilets of light. Now it coruscates with gold; now it deepens into honey-coloured shadows; now it is raven black; now it reflects the blue flower-tints of a dove's throat. And then when it has been anointed with Arabian nard, or parted by the fine teeth of the artful comb, or looped up at the nape of the neck, the lover looks upon it, sees there his own face, as in a mirror, enhanced by delight. O what beauty in Hair, whether in braided luxuriance it is twisted together and built up upon the head, or whether it is allowed to tumble in prolix curls down the back. Such, I conclude, is the dignity of Hair that no woman whosoever, though dressed-up with gold, tissues, gems, and all other cosmetical apparatus, could be described, unless she had duly arranged her hair, as dressed at all.

But as far as my Fotis was concerned, it was not toilet-care but ringleted freedom that crowned her charms. Her plentiful hair, thrown loosely back and hanging down to her nape, was scattered over her shoulders and rested softly upon the swelling fringes of her dress, till at last it was gently collected and fastened up by a knot on the top of her head.

I could no longer bear the excruciation of such exquisite pleasure, and bending forwards I impressed a most delicious kiss on the spot where the hair was heaped on the crown of her head. She twisted away and looked at me over her shoulder with sidelong and marrow-sucking glances.

'Hey now, my scholar,' she said, 'sweet and bitter is the sauce you lick. Take care that the sweetness of an overdose of honey doesn't choke you bitterly with bile for many a fine day.'

'How is that, my Merriment?' I asked. 'I am ready to be laid flat for basting above that fire as long as I am recruited every while by a tiny kiss.' And, as good as my word, I embraced her more straitly and began kissing her.

With that her own desires kindled and a mutually waxing ardour twined our bodies akin in love. Cinnamon was the exhalation of her opening mouth; and she succumbed to my kiss, while her quickening tongue nectarously ravished me.

'I am going,' I said. 'No, I'm a gone man already, unless you take pity on me.'

Repeating the exploit of her kiss, she answered: 'Raise up your spirits, man. I am fettered to you by the same leg-cuff of desire, and our pleasures won't be delayed very much longer. At the first flicker of torchtime I shall be in your bedroom. So be off, and gird yourself ready, for I mean to have a nightlong bone to pick with you, and there'll be no flinching on my side.' And so, after some further (similarly pointed) remarks, we parted for the moment.

56. AFTER-LUNCH APPEAL

Catullus

Sweet Ipsithilla, see me soon,
O be a dear, you sweet young thing,
ask me to visit you at noon.
If yes it is, don't change once more
and bid some servant bar the door;
and don't rush out to call or shop,
but nicely wait for what I'll bring,
and then – nine hugs without a stop!
So, if you're home, at once reply.
I've lunched and sprawling here I lie
with tunic monstrously awry.

57. POLICE OFFICIALS IN DISGRACE

Aulus Gellius

HOSTILIUS MANCINUS was a high police official.
He laid a charge against the prostitute Manilia before
the assembly of the people, alleging that at night he'd
been struck by a stone thrown from her apartment, and
he put his wound in as evidence.

Manilia appealed to the tribunes of the commons.
She made a statement that Mancinus had come along
to her house all dressed up for a night out, but it didn't
happen to be convenient for her to let him in. So he

tried to crash the door down and had to be driven off with stones.

The tribunes decided that the policeman had been rightly refused admittance to a place where it wasn't at all respectable for him to go with a garland of flowers on his head. They therefore quashed his action.

58. SOME JOKES

'What do you think of a man caught in adultery?'
'He's very slow.'

*　　　*　　　*

'Who's that?'
'My wife.'
'By God, she's like you too.'

*　　　*　　　*

A Sicilian, hearing a friend lament that his wife had hanged herself on a fig-tree, said: 'Do please give me a slip of that tree to plant at home.'

59. PLEASURE GROUND

Ovid

This day with genial Anna we must pass.
Near wandering Tiber is her pleasure ground.
The crowd stroll out and sprawl about the grass,
drink wine and lie in loving couples round.

Some own the sky and some have brought a tent,
some splice a hut with boughs entwined and spread,
some use the reeds for frame and are content
to lay a cloak or mantle overhead.

They glow with sun and wine – to live, they vow,
as many years as cups compose the feast.
That man has drunk himself a Nestor now,
that wench will be a Sibyl at the least.

They hum or sing a catchy theatre-song
with naughty gestures merrily in keeping.
They drink and dance in gawky rows along,
with straying hair the prinked-up piece goes leaping.

Then home they totter, drunk. All eyes they draw.
The watchers bless them and their field-carouse.
I met them lately. This is what I saw:
a tipsy crone who dragged her tipsy spouse.

[*On the festival of Anna Perenna, the Turn of the Year,
15 March: the people gathered in what was Rome's
Hampstead Heath.*]

60. SHEPHERDS' MEETING

Calpurnius Siculus

Iollas. Hey, Lycidas, seen a heifer of mine by any chance. She often slinks off to get in the way of your bulls? I've wasted nearly two hours chasing her, and not a glimpse. Kept on hurting my legs on this spiky broom, paid no heed to all the scratches from the thick brambles, but I've lost blood and gained nought.

Lycidas. I don't know, I wasn't watching, I've no time. I'm burned-up, with nothing to damp me down, Iollas, burned-up. Phyllis has dodged off, not a drop of gratitude. She's hooked a new lover, Mopsus, spite of all the presents I dropped in her lap.

Iollas. Ah, woman's changeable as the winds. So that's how it goes with your Phyllis. Why, I remember, when you weren't there, she swore honey itself was bitter in her mouth.

Lycidas. You'll hear my whole moan, Iollas, when you've got a spare moment. Search those willows now, take a turn under the elms on the left. When the meadows are sweltering, my bull likes resting there, stretching out big in the cool shade and cud-chewing after the morning's graze.

Iollas. No, friend, though you jeer at me, I won't go. Here, Tityrus boy, get off on your own to those willows he said, and if you do find the heifer there, grab her, bring her back this way with shower of blows. But don't forget to fetch your broken crook too. Come on now, Lycidas, out with it. What mighty brawl has given you such a body blow? What god sliddered in to snap your love?

Lycidas. I never wanted anyone but Phyllis, you'll back up my words, Iollas, so I turned down Callirhoe with a bump, though she came begging with dowry and all. Then what happens but Phyllis starts letting Mopsus help her fit some reeds together with wax, and there she is, singing under the oaktree with that clod at her side. When I saw what was going on, I admit it, I felt so burned-up inside I couldn't take a bit more. I went straight and tore both her vests wide open, I beat her on the naked breasts. In a rage she dashed off to Alcippe, and as she went she called out, 'All right, you dirtydog, your Phyllis is leaving you and taking up with Mopsus.' And now she's staying in Alcippe's house and I'm scared they won't open up to me. But even more than wanting to get her back, I'm panting to see her break off from Mopsus.

Iollas. It was you started the quarrel. So you must be the one to put out your hands first and cave in. Even when a girl's to blame, it's only right to humour her. If you want to send a message, I'm your man to take it and do my level best to win the ear of your rampaging sweetheart.

Lycidas. I've been giving a lot of thought to the sort of song I'll use to quiet her down. Maybe she'll be more amenable when she hears a ditty. She always praises my pieces skyhigh.

Iollas. Come on, say it. I'll carve your words on cherry-bark, then cut out the bit with the words on and take it along.

Lycidas (singing):

I'm sending these prayers in the wan of my grief,
    this song from the night of my sighs.
There's a tear in my eye as I stand singing here

and sleep's whisht away from my eyes.
So scraggy's no thrush when the olivetree's stript,
    no hare, when the last grape is gone,
as I who go pining for Phyllis my darling,
    resignedly wandering on.
Alas, with you lost, all the lilies are black
    as wasting in sorrow I sink.
There's no taste at all to be traced in the spring,
    and brackish the wine that I drink.
But if you come back, there's white in the lilies,
    and water and wine taste aright.
For I am the fellow you tenderly kisst
    in whose songs you declared much delight.

That boaster may chat about gifts made of gold,
    but sad stuff like lupines he gleans
in the black of the night and makes up for the lack
    of bread by the boiling of greens.
He calls himself happy and heavenly-blest
    when on his bare table he finds
the chaff of coarse barley that in a crackt mill
    with his own hands he clumsily grinds.
Come on, Iollas, if you're the chap to help someone
who's given up the ghost, take that along and plead with
her as tunefully as you can. I'll stand on one side, hidden
maybe by the prickly reedgrass or crouched near under
the garden-hedge.

Iollas. I'm off, and she'll come, unless I read fate all
wrong. For look over there, Tityrus has brought me a
cheerful omen. He's done it, he's found my heifer.

61. SPELLS ON LEADEN TABLETS

I DELIVER to you that you may send a demon into her and other spirits from below so that she won't despise me any longer but do whatever I want Vettia whose mother is Optata so I call on your help because through my love I can't sleep nor swallow bread nor meat I bind Vettia whose mother is Optata in sense and intelligence and mind and will so that she will love me Felix whose mother is Fructa from this day from this hour that she will forget her father and her mother and all her relations and all her friends and the love of all other men but me Felix whose mother is Fructa till she Vettia whose mother is Optata has only me in her mind sleeping or waking whether she is hot or cold let Vettia whose mother is Optata burn for love and desire of me.

*　　　*　　　*

You gods of hell I give her up to you if you have any sangtitty and I hand across to you Tychine of Carisius whatever she does let it go wrong all ways round you gods of hell I give her up to you all her body her complexion her figure her head her hairs her shadow her chin her lips her mouth her breathing her throat her liver her shoulders her heart her lungs her intrails her belly her arms her fingers her hands her navel her bowels her thighs her legs her heels her coles her toes you gods of hell if I see her wasting off I will sure make you sacrifices every year I give you my oath you holy parent ones may waste off all up her.

[These are genuine curses devoting Vettia and Tychine to the Underworld.]

62. THE RIVAL

Catullus

If ever there was man who justly stank
and paid for lust with gout in every limb,
the man who's lying by my mistress's flank
is he. For both afflictions meet in him.

Thus I'm revenged each time they meet abed;
she's pale with nausea and with gout he's dead.

63. VARIOUS CHARACTERS

Luxorius

Myrto selects the girls who are ugly-faced,
and when he sees a pretty girl, he blenches.
Speak, Myrto: do you choose in beastly taste,
not northern blondes but southern darkie-wenches?
But no, I pardon you for what you miss.
Only the ugly ones will take your kiss.

*   *   *

You're hairy-limbed and hairy-faced,
long-bearded to look reverend:
a Stoic Master, loudly chaste,
austerely all your days you spend.
You'd never say that you could bend
to wenches, or you'd be disgraced.
But vigils all the night you spend
with lovely girls who get no sleep:
Cato by day, discreetly stern,
at night an incubus you turn.

*   *   *

Who wins Marina's love may surely claim
he's gone a deep-sea voyage rollingly.
But we should rather compliment than blame:
Venus, was born, remember, from the sea.

64. DINNER CONVERSATIONS

Petronius

A PRIEST'S attendant knocked on the dining-room door, and a man robed in white for some festivity came in with a mob of friends. I was confounded by his lordly air and thought it was a judge of the bench who'd looked in. So I did my best to stagger up and set my bare feet on the floor.

Agamemnon laughed at my confusion. 'Hold yourself in, you simpleton,' he said. 'It's only Habinnas, priest of Augustus and stonemason. Said to make the choicest tombstones in town.'

Relieved at the information, I sank back on my couch and watched the entry of Habbinas with unabated astonishment. He was already quite tight and had his hands draped over his wife's shoulders. He had several wreaths piled on his head and perfumes were running down his forehead into his eyes. He sat in the chief seat (lowest on the middle couch) and immediately called for wine and hot water.

His joviality pleased our host Trimalchio, who demanded a large cup for himself and asked what sort of time his new guest had been having.

'Everything in the world,' Habinnas hiccoughed, 'only not you. I'd left my eyes behind here. Yes, my oath, they did us proud. Scissa was giving a ninth-day wake for her poor dear slave. She set him free after he was dead. Colossal death duties to pay, so I hear. They reckon he died worth fifty thousand. All the same, she put on a good show, even if we did have to slop half the drinks over his lamented bones.'

'Yes,' said Trimalchio, 'but tell us the menu.'

'I'll recite it,' said Habinnas, 'if I can. I've got such a good memory I often forget even my own name. Well, let me see. First we had a pig crowned with a winecup. Garnished with honeycakes and giblets – just done right – and beetroot of course, and wholemeal bread, absolutely pure. I'd rather have it than that white-looking stuff. It builds up your strength. And for myself, when I go to do my business, I've no complaints. O, and the next dish was a cold tart, served with warm honey and a first-rate Spanish wine poured over it. I took a big bite into that tart and I did myself well with the honey. Side-dishes of pease and lupins, a choice of nuts, and an apple per man. All the same I got away with two and here I have them knotted in my napkin. Because if I didn't take something nice back for that pet slave of mine he'd kick up hell's delight. O yes, my wife's reminding me. On the sideboard was a joint of bear's meat. Scintilla was rash enough to have a taste and she almost spewed her guts up. I ate over a pound myself, and it tasted just like wild boar. What I say is, if a bear eats up us poor men, how much more right has a poor man to eat a bear? To round things off, we had cheese ripened in new wine, and snails all round, and helpings of tripe, and liver in little dishes, and eggs with caps on, and turnips, and mustard, and forcemeat rissoles – but pish Palamedes! Pickled olives too were handed round in a bowl and some greedyguts took three handfuls. For we'd let the ham pass unscathed. But tell me, Caius, why isn't Fortunata at dinner?'

'You know what she is,' Trimalchio replied. 'Until she's counted all the silver and shared out all the left-overs among the slaves, she won't even wet her lips with water.'

'All right,' said Habinnas, 'unless she comes and takes her place, I'll skedaddle.'

He was making a start at rising up when at a given signal all the slaves yelled out 'Fortunata' four times and more. So she came along. She was wearing a high yellow sash, which didn't hide her cherry-red petticoat, her spiral anklets and her white slippers embroidered in gold. She wiped her hands on a napkin hanging round her neck, took her place on the sofa where Scintilla, Habinnas' wife, was stretched out. Scintilla welcomed her effusively and Fortunata gave her a kiss. 'It's a treat, my dear, to see you.'

After a while they got so confidential that Fortunata was wrenching the bracelets off her fat arms and show-ing them to Scintilla to admire. In the end she even removed her anklets and her hairnet, which she said was made of pure gold.

Trimalchio saw what she was doing, and asked for the heap of jewellery to be brought to him. 'Look at them,' he said. 'Women's fetters, that's what they are. You see how us fatheads are ruined. She must have six and a half pounds of gold on her. I myself, I admit, have got an armlet on that weighs all of ten pounds. I made it out of the thousandth per cent I offer up to Mercury out of all my transactions.' He wouldn't let the subject drop, and to prove his words he ordered scales to be fetched and handed the ring round for us all to check the weight.

Scintilla was just as bad. She slipped a small gold locket from her neck. Her Luck she called it. Then she produced two ear-rings and gave them one after the other to Fortunata for inspection, saying, 'He's so generous, my lord and master. Nobody's got stones so fine.'

'O yes,' said Habinnas, 'you made me gust bust buying you a glass bean. It's a fact, if I had a daughter I'd snip off her ears. Everything would be dirt-cheap if it wasn't for women. As it is, it's a matter of drinking cold and passing it out hot.'

The sozzled ladies, ignoring him, went on laughing together and sprawling in drunken kisses. One boasted what an economical housewife she was; the other chatted about her husband's pets and how he had no time for her. While they were thus wrapped up in one another, Habinnas got stealthily up, grabbed Fortunata by the legs and tipped her over on the sofa. She screamed *au au* as her dress went up past her knees. Taking refuge in Scintilla's bosom, she hid her fiery blushes in her napkin.

Soon after this, Trimalchio ordered the second instalment of the dinner to be brought in. The slaves carried out all the tables, fetched a fresh supply, and scattered sawdust tinged with saffron and vermilion. Also, what was a new thing for me, powdered mica. Trimalchio promptly remarked, 'I really think I might have been satisfied with the course we've had. But I see you've got a fresh lot there. So let's have it, if you've got something nice.'

Meanwhile a boy from Alexandria, who was taking hot water round, began imitating a nightingale, and Trimalchio broke in periodically, 'Change the tune!'

Then another diversion came up. The slave who sat at Habinnas' feet – bidden, I suppose, by his master – began suddenly shouting in a sort of drone: 'Now with his fleet Aeneas held the main . . .' No shriller sound ever punctuated my eardrums. Besides making barbarous errors in intonation, in raising and lowering his voice, the fellow interpolated fragments out of the ancient Italian farces, so that Virgil for the first time in my life got on my nerves. That didn't stop Habinnas giving him a clap when he at last halted. 'Never went to school,' he said. 'I educated him by sending him round to listen to the quacks in the market. So he's absolutely on his own at an imitation of muleteers and mountebanks. Damnably smart, that's him. He's a cobbler too, and a cook, and a confectioner, a jack of all trades. Only got two faults, and if he could rid himself of those he'd be the world's best. He's circumcised and he snores. That he's cross-eyed I don't hold against him. We know Venus squints. So now you see why he can't keep silent and hardly ever closes an eye. I bought him for three hundred denars.'

Here Scintilla interrupted his chatter. 'Yes, but you're not mentioning all the artful dodges of this wretch of a slave. Anyone with half an eye could guess that. But I'll see that the creature gets branded.'

Trimalchio gave a laugh. 'Ha, I smell out the Cappadocian. Habinnas doesn't deny himself, and on my oath I praise him for it. For that's something they won't send on with him at the funeral. Take my word for it, we know you women too. By my hope of salvation, I used to have a go at the missus, until the master got a smell of it and sent me off to run a place in the country. But hush, my tongue. I'll stuff some bread into you.'

The rascally slave, as if he'd been commended highly, took a clay lamp out from under his shirt and imitated trumpeters for more than half an hour. All the while Habinnas pulled down his lower lip and sang in accompaniment. As a final touch the slave swaggered out into the middle of the room, took off flute-players with the aid of clattering reeds, or treated us to the Muleteer's Lot, with cloak and whip. At length Habinnas called him over, gave him a kiss, and offered him a drink. 'Better than ever, Massa,' he said; 'you've earned a pair of hobnails.'

The agony would have gone on and on if the last course hadn't now arrived, thrushes moulded of fine dough and packed with raisins and nuts. Quinces came next, bristling all over with thorns to look like hedgehogs. But now our high spirits got their knock-back. A rather handsome lad had come in with the new waiters. Trimalchio took a fancy to him and wouldn't leave him alone. So Fortunata, to assert her wifely rights and keep even with her husband, began abusing him and called him a stinker and shocker for making a show of himself in company. At last she worked herself up to screaming at him as a 'low hound'.

Trimalchio took offence at her harangue and in reply let her have a cup full in the face. She gave a screech as if her eye had gone, and lifted up her trembling hands to her face. Scintilla too was in a scare and drew her shuddering friend into her arms. An obliging slave held a cool little water jug against her cheek, and Fortunata, leaning over it, began moaning and weeping.

'What's all this fuss?' Trimalchio cried. 'This nightclub tart has lost her memory, eh? And I took her off the sale-platform and made her an honest woman! But she puffs up like a bullfrog. She's too good to spit in her own bosom for luck. A wooden block, not a woman. But if you were born in a mud hut, you can't sleep in a proper house. So help me, my guardian spirit, but I'll tame this Cassandra in topboots. And I might have married ten million, stupid that I was. You know I'm telling the exact truth. Agatho, the beauty-expert of the rich

134

woman next door, she took me aside and said to me: "Take my advice and don't let your family die out." But just because I act the gentleman and don't want to look fickle, I stick the axe into my own leg. All right, I'll make you come after me with your claws. Get it into your thick skull straightaway what harm you've done yourself. Habinnas, don't put any statue of her on my tomb or else I'll have her nagging at me when I'm dead. And to let her know how ruthless I can be, I won't let her kiss me after I'm laid out.'

When this thunderbolt had been launched, Habinnas intervened with pleas for moderation in anger. 'We've all got our faults,' he observed. 'We're men, not gods.' Scintilla wept and said the same. She called Trimalchio Caius and begged him by his Genius to unbend.

He couldn't hold back his own tears. 'Habinnas, please,' he said, 'as you hope to enjoy your own money, spit in my face if I've done a thing wrong. I kissed that good little boy, not because he's a good-looker but because he's such a good little boy. He can do division sums and read books at sight, and he's bought a suit of Thracian armour out of his day-wages. Yes, he's acquired a round-backed chair out of his own savings, and two ladles. Isn't he the right sort for me to keep my eyes on? But Fortunata says no. Is that the way you feel, madam high-heels? I advise you to stick to the good things you've got in your own cooking-pot, you vulture, you. Don't make me show my fangs, you darling little thing. You know what I am. When once I've made up my mind, it's fixed with a ten-inch nail. But it's time we came back to the living. Make yourselves at home, friends, that's all I ask. I was once no better than you yourselves, but I'd qualities that got me where I am. Brains is what makes men, the rest's all trash. I buy well, I sell well. Some folks will tell you different. But look at me, I'm bursting with what it takes.

'Hey, now there, you snuffler, still at your whines? I'll soon give you something real to whine about. But as I was saying, it's thrift that brought me the fortune I have. When I came out of Asia, I was about as tall as this candlestick. In fact I used to measure against it, every day, and rub oil from the lamp round my lips to make my beard sprout. Still, I was my master's pet for fourteen years. Nothing wrong in obeying the master. And I gave his wife what she wanted too. You know what I mean. I'll leave it at that. No one can say I'm the sort that boasts.

'Anyway, as the gods willed, I became the real master in the house and the other fellow hadn't any thoughts he could call his own. You can guess the rest. I was named joint-heir with Caesar and I came into an estate good enough for a senator. But a man's not satisfied with nothing. I got a passion for trade. I won't keep you long. I built five ships, put a cargo of wine in – wine was worth its weight in gold at the time – and set off for Rome. You might think I'd fixed the whole thing. Every ship was wrecked; a fact, I'm not romancing. Neptune swallowed thirty million in one day. But do you think I was downhearted? Heavens, no; I no more kept the taste of the loss in my system than if it had never happened. I built another fleet, bigger, better, with a larger layout. No one could say I didn't have pluck. You know, a big ship has got a big sort of strength about it. I put in another cargo of wine, bacon, beans, perfumes, slaves. And here's where Fortunata showed the stuff she's made of. She sold all her jewellery, all her clothes, and put a hundred gold pieces in my hand. That was the leaven that made my fortune rise. When the gods give a push, things happen quick. I turned in a cool ten million from the one trip. Straight-off I bought up all the estates that had been my master's. I built a mansion and bought slaves and cattle. Whatever I touched, grew like honeycomb. When I came to have more than all the revenues of the land of my birth, I dropped speculation. Retired from direct trade, and went for financing freedmen.

'I was feeling like I'd never want to be mixed up in any more business deals, but I was given new heart by an astrologer who happened along to our town, a little Greek chap named Serapa. In the councils of the gods he was. He told me things about myself that even I'd forgotten. Explained everything from needle-and-thread upwards. Knew my very bowels, he did, and the only thing he couldn't tell me was what I'd had for dinner the day before. You'd have thought he'd been a kind of shadow to me. You remember, Habinnas – you were there, weren't you? – he says to me: "You picked up your wife in a what-do-you-call-'em, you're not lucky in your friends, nobody's ever as grateful as you deserve, you're a big landowner, you're feeding a viper under your wing." And he says too, though this is something I mustn't mention, I've got even now thirty years, four months, and two days left. What's more, I'll soon come into a legacy. My oracle tells me so. If I could only extend my estates to Apulia. I'd have got enough for this life. And in the meantime, while Mercury watched over me, I built this house. As you know, at first it was only a cottage. Now it's fit to stick a god in. Four dining-rooms, twenty bedrooms, two marble colonnades, an upstairs dining-room, a bedroom where I sleep myself, this viper's boudoir, and a superb porter's lodge. Plenty of accommodation for guests. In fact when Scaurus was here, he wouldn't put up anywhere else, and he's got a family-place on the seaside. There's a mile of other

things I'll show you in a moment. Believe me, if you
have a penny, you're worth a penny. The more you have,
the more you are. So your friend who was once the Frog
is now the Prince.'

65. CURSE ON A FORTUNE-TELLING BAWD

Tibullus

May blood be mingled with her food and foul
her lips that turn to gall the sweetest wines.
May ghosts about her always sway and howl
while on the roof the vampire shrilly whines.

Delirious, may she root for graveyard-herbs
and gnaw the bones that wolves refused to eat.
And when, bare-loined and shrieking, she disturbs
a village, may curs chase her down the street.

66. JULIUS CAESAR

Suetonius

THE only blot on his chastity was his relations with King Nicomedes. But that one episode stuck to him all his life and exposed him to much merciless raillery. I shall not linger on the famous lines of Calvus Licinius:

Whatever Bithynia and her Lord possessed,
her Lord by whom was Caesar well caressed

I skip the speeches of Dolabella and the elder Curio — the former calling him the Queen's Rival and Innerside of the Royal Couch, and the latter, the Brothel of Nicomedes or the Bithynian Stews. I also omit the edicts of Bibulus when he was Caesar's colleague, which libellously cite him as the Queen of Bithynia, adding that 'once he was in love with a King, but now he covets a Kingdom'. About that time as M. Brutus tells us, one Octavius, a fellow with a crazed brain and therefore all the freer in his abusive witticisms, addressed Pompey in a crowded assembly by the title of King and then went on to hail Caesar as Queen. C. Memmius also upbraided him with serving the King at table, among the rest of his catamites, in the presence of a numerous company which included merchants from Rome — he gives the names. But Cicero was not satisfied with describing in some of his letters how Caesar was led by the royal attendants into the King's bed-chamber, put into a bed of gold with a covering of purple, and how the youthful bloom of this scion of Venus had been corrupted in

Bithynia. When Caesar was pleading the cause of Nicomedes' daughter, Nysa, before the Senate, and mentioning the King's kindnesses, he, Cicero, butted in: 'Come
on, please tell us more of that. It's well known what he
gave you and you gave him.'

67. SONGS OF THE SOLDIERS AT THE TRIUMPH OF G. JULIUS CAESAR

Caesar, he bent to Nicomedes,
  The Gauls to Caesar now bend.
Caesar made the Gauls bend down
  and Triumphs at the end.
Nicomedes gets no Triumph,
  yet he made Ceasar bend.

*   *   *

On the girls of Gaul you made your splash.
Hard-up you've come to raise more cash.

*   *   *

Ho, watch your wives, you men of Rome.
We bring the bald-head lecher home.

68. AGAINST CAESAR AND HIS CHIEF ENGINEER

Catullus

Well the base pair in dirt agree,
Caesar, Mamurra, he or she,
divide a blotched equality,
a Roman and a Formian:
the stains go deep in either man.
As twins or rottenness, they share
one dilettante sofa-lair,
so wildly wenching as to be
allied rivals in their lechery.

Well the base pair in dirt agree.

*   *   *

I greet you, snubnosed lady, who
own shapeless ankles, pallid eyes,
wet lips and fingers stubbed in size,
a tongue that's unrefined in haste,
the Formian bankrupt's mistress too.
Provincials hand you beauty's prize
and call you Lesbia's rival, you.

O, how this witless age lacks taste.

*   *   *

Yes, used-up Ameana begs
a cool ten thousand out of me.
With minimal nose and wonky legs,
the Formian bankrupt's piece is she.

Hey, you that have wench in charge,
call doctors while she's yet at large.
She's mad. I diagnose her case:
Delusions of the Mirror-face.

*   *   *

Whose eye can view this thing and not be blinded
except a gambling glutton basely minded?
Far Britons and the long-haired Gauls have grieved
for pocket-money that Mamurra thieved.

You pervert Romulus, don't you see the game,
you gluttonous gambler basely lost to shame?
Speak, shall the cocksure braggart wield the rod
and make a town of wives obey his nod
like a white treading-pigeon or a god?

You pervert Romulus, don't you care a button,
you basely-minded gambler turned a glutton?
Is this why you went westward wandering,
that flaccid Cockerel, anxious to be dirty,
should waste some twenty millions odd, or thirty?

What matter figures to such evil generosity?
Not ruinous yet enough his impecuniosity?
His patrimony first was lewdly lost,
his Pontic money next. To meet the cost
Spain next paid cash from Tagus' golden streams,
and now the Gauls and Britons have bad dreams.

Why then support the beast? You'll learn too late,
at every meal he swallows an estate.
Yet you and Son-in-law, you mates of might,
consume the City's powers to bloat such blight.

[*Mamurra of Formiae was Caesar's efficient Chief of
Engineers. In the winter of 55–54* B.C., *during the Gallic
War, Caesar and his staff had retired to Verona, Catullus'
home-town. There Mamurra and Catullus had some
clash. Mamurra is 'Cockerel'; Caesar is the 'pervert Romulus'; 'Son-in-law' is Pompey with whom Caesar was still
in accord.*]

69. AUGUSTUS CAESAR

Suetonius

EVEN his friends do not deny that he could be accused
of various acts of adultery; but in his defences they
allege that his motive for intriguing with women was not
desire but policy – he wanted to pry into the designs of
his opponents through their wives. Marc Antony, besides noting his headlong marriage with Livia, charges
him with leading the wife of a man of consular rank
from the dinner-table into a bedroom, with her husband looking on – and then bringing her back with her
ears very red and hair all over the place. He also declares
that he divorced Scribonia for resenting too loudly the
influence gained over him by one of his mistresses and
that his friends were compelled to pimp for him.
Matrons and virgins ripe for marriage were in consequence obliged to strip bare for an over-all examination of their persons, just as if Thornaius, the slave-

dealer, was putting them up for sale. And before the rupture occurred between Antony and Augustus, the former wrote to him in a familiar strain:

'Why are you changed towards me? Because I have a Queen in my bed? After all, she's my wife. And is it a new thing on my part or haven't I done it nightly these nine years? Yourself, do you take freedoms with Drusilla only? May health and happiness be yours according to the extent you're not dallying (as you read these words) with Tertulla, Terentilla, Rufilla, or Salvia Titiscenia – or with the whole lot in a bunch. What does it matter to you where or on whom you expend that manly vigour of yours?'

Augustus gave a private party (commonly called the Supper of the Twelve Gods) at which the guests were dressed up in the costumes of gods and goddesses. He himself took the role of Apollo. This episode caused much scandal. Not only does Antony bring it up in his letters, giving the names of all the persons concerned, but the following anonymous lines were circulated:

When lately at a dinner-masquerade
Twelve Gods in well-matched pairs had Mallia puzzl-
ing,
The part of Phoebus Caesar vilely played:
in new adulteries the gods lay guzzling.
From earth depart the outraged Deities
and from his golden throne Jove, angry, flies.

70. THE FABULOUS LADIES

Lucilius

That famous lady with beautiful ankles
and beautiful ringlets of hair,
do you think it was expressly forbidden
to touch her anywhere?

And she whom Amphitryon took to bed,
as others did at their ease,
wasn't she bandy in the legs
and knocking at the knees?

And Leda herself, the wonderful woman,
the swan-white bride of a bird,
I leave you to find out the sort she was:
choose a one-syllable word.

And highborn Tyro, did she possess
a wart upon her snout,
a hairy mole, or at the least
a tooth projecting out?

71. LOSER

Propertius

Laugh, lovely one. You'd sorrow if another
were lovelier, and your pride need never sigh.

But you that snared her, may your wife's damned
      mother
infest you. May her father never die.

If you have thieved a bounteous night or two,
she came from hate of me, not love of you.

72. SUBTLE INSULT

Catullus

Come from all sides, my couplet crew,
here, in a bustle, all of you!
A wicked wench has set her wit
to mock at me. Will you submit?

She stole my notebook. I demand:
follow and snatch it from her hand.

Which girl? That one ahead, who trips
with obvious waggle of the hips,
and grinning like a Gallic hound.
Go shouting as you ring her round:
    You slut and crook, restore the book,
    restore, you slut, the book, you crook.

She gives no sign. What words defile?
    Hey, you whole brothelful of guile,
    you shan't escape, you lump of dirt.
We'll make her blush, we'll somehow hurt
the broad face of this brazen bitch.
So clamour in a louder pitch:
    You whore, restore the book you took,
    you whore and crook, restore the book.

She takes no notice. It's in vain.
Then try if there's a subtler strain
which may successfully upbraid:
    Chaste virgin, give it back, pure maid.

73. MISDIRECTED TRAVELLER

Petronius

I WAS listening so intently to the professor that I didn't notice Ascyltos had given me the slip. And I was pacing up and down the gardens in the heat of our discussion when a large mob of students came jostling into the porch, apparently from some master or other whose extemporary declamation had been given after Agamemnon's discourse. While the young fellows were ridiculing his fine turns of phrase and tearing the general tendency of his style to shreds, I seized the chance of making off and departed in a hurry after Ascyltos.

But I didn't remember the way at all accurately, nor did I know where our inn was. So wherever I wandered, I kept coming back to where I started, till I was worn out with walking and dripped with sweat. At last I approached an old girl who was hawking country-vegetables, and said to her, 'Please, mother, I don't suppose you can tell me where I'm lodging?'

She was charmed by my polite idiocy. 'Of course I can,' she replied, stood up, and proceeded to lead the way. I took her to be a witch. But after a while, when we'd come to an out-of-the-way corner, the obliging old thing threw back a patchwork curtain and remarked, 'That ought to be your home.'

I was insisting that I didn't recall the place when I caught a glimpse of some men and naked trollops strolling stealthily about among cells with price-tickets. Slowly, in fact far too late, I realized that I had been decoyed into a mollshop. With a curse on the old hag's trickery, I covered up my head and ran through the midst of the brothel in the other direction. And there, almost on the threshold, I bumped into Ascyltos, as fagged-out as myself and giving up the ghost. He looked as if he'd been lured along by the same old woman. I greeted him with a grin and asked him what business he had in such a disreputable hole. He wiped his sweat off with his hands, and said, 'If you only knew what happened to me.'

'What's the story?' I asked.

'I was wandering about all over the town,' he answered in a faint voice, 'but I couldn't locate our lodgings. Then a respectable-looking chap came up and most politely offered to show me the way. He promptly plunged down into a lot of shady twists and turns, and dumped me down here, then began offering me cash down. What's worse, a tart extorted threepence out of me for a room, and that guide of mine was getting obstreperous. Luckily I had enough strength in my arms to teach him a lesson. And then you came along.'

74. TO AN AMOROUS AND UNATTRACTIVE LADY

Horace

Destined to mate black trumpeting elephants, explain
   your drift.
My kisses you'll not lure with note or gift.
Pick out some stalwart chap, I say, whose hasty tastes are
   low.
For with my most sagacious nose I know
where polyp-growths or armpit-goats are lurking, long
   before
the slickest hound can scent a hidden boar.

O, how she sweats with miasmatic efforts like a tumbler,
yet at the end remains as much a grumbler,
despite her fierce effluvia. Her damp solicitude
wipes paint and powder off, and leaves her hued
like ordure of a crocodile, till, tears of fury shedding,
she raps the bedstead and she rips the bedding.

Then she attacks my shrinking ways and slangs me
   angrily.
'You're better with Inachia than me.
You go on for three times with her, but here you're always
   stuck.
Not once a gentleman. May wretched luck
strike Lesbia who guaranteed you'd prove a hardy lad.
And there's Amyntas that I could have had,
a chap who's always up to the high watermark of hope,
like a young sapling cleaving to its slope.

'For whom were worked the fleeces of the richest Tyrian
   dye?
For you, you'll say. That's not what I'd reply.
At any party there's no wife who would not choose to hug,
rather than you, her husband. Yes, you slug.
O what a fate. Am I a wolf that you, a lamb, should fear
   me?
a lion, that a goatbitch can't come near me?'

75. ON HAIR-DYE GONE WRONG

Ovid

N o w didn't I keep on telling you, 'Leave off messing round with your hair?' And now you've simply got no hair left to try out all your dyeing nonsense on. Admit, if you'd only left it alone, what woman had a thicker head of hair? It used to hang right down your sides, just as long as you are yourself. And what's more, wasn't it so fine in texture that you were afraid to curl it with tongs, just like those delicate silks the Chinese weave? or like the thread that the spider draws out with her thin legs when she fastens her frail web under the neglected beam? And yet its colour wasn't black, it wasn't golden, it was a mixture of the two. A hue like that of the lofty cedar in the damp valleys of cragged Ida, when the bark is stript off.

And what's more, it was tractable, that lost hair of yours was. It fell naturally into a thousand little ringlets and didn't give you the least trouble. Neither the bodkin you used to part it, nor the tooth of the comb, ever did it the least damage. Your tire-woman always had a clear skin, you didn't pinch her for causing you pain. Many a time I've sat and watched your head being dressed; and not once did I see you grab the bodkin and stab the girl in the arms, as I've seen other women do. Many a time in the morning, before you had your hair done, I've watched you lying stretched-out on the purple couch, with your face half upturned. And even then, without the least toilet, how lovely you were – like a Thracian Bacchanal who, tired with the dance, sprawls with careless legs on the green grass. And yet, for all its fineness, its softness, what endless torments did you impose upon it. How patiently it had to submit to the iron and the fire, all to gain an extra-crispness for the curls in their twists and tendril-turns.

'What a shame,' I used to cry, 'what a shame to go burning and drying up that hair. At least, you cruel-hearted woman, have some pity on your own head. Drop all this violent treatment. Your hair doesn't deserve to be scorched. Why, your locks know better than the intrusive bodkin how to lie in order to look most delightful.'

And now those beautiful locks are all gone, locks that Apollo might have envied and Bacchus might have coveted for his own head. They reminded me of that famous picture in which Venus stands naked from the bath, holding her long hair up with her dripping hand. What are you complaining of now that you've lost the hair you used to maltreat? Why, you silly, do you lay down the mirror with unconsolable hand? You don't look so good to eyes accustomed to a different image. If you want to please, forget the thing you were.

No magical herbs of a rival have done you this injury. No treacherous hag has been washing you with corrosive fluids. And you're not suffering from the after-effects of some disease – touch wood. No envious tongue has thinned your abundant tresses, no glint of the evil eye. It was your own self that prepared and poured the caustic poison on your head. Now Germany will be sending you her captured locks, and you'll be adorned once more, thanks to a conquered race. Ah, how many times you'll have to blush as some admire your wig and think it your own hair. You'll murmur to yourself, 'Now I am getting the praises that belong by rights to a bought commodity. It's not me he's complimenting, it's some Sigambrian girl whose hair I wear, a girl I've never seen. Still, I recall the time when the glory of my head was all my own.'

Wretch that I am, it's all she can do to stop from bursting into tears. Her pretty cheeks are warm with blushes and she covers her face with her hand. She ventures to peep at her former tresses, which she's placed in her bosom—a treasure, alas, that hardly suits that pleasant spot.

Calm your feelings, calm your features. The loss isn't irreparable. Before long your hair will grow again and restore your natural beauty.

76. EGNATIUS FROM SPAIN

Catullus

Lewd Clubhouse and you wallowing scum
(nine posts from the Capped Brothers) come!
You're the sole virile chaps, you think;
you think you own each bit of skirt,
and we are goats to treat like dirt.
You hundred or two hundred fools,
I'll see your towering ardour cools.
Alone I'll make it burst and sink.

You laugh? I warn you, smirk no more.
I'll scribble scorpions round the door
where she I love (who ran from me,
loved as no other woman yet:
for whom I've battled mightily)
keeps open house.
            You tight bright set,
you love her, often. How it pains,
you petty puddlers in backlanes,
and you, worst of the long-haired lot,
whom rabbit-riddled Spain begot,
Egnatius, wretchedly endeared
with stale-scrubbed teeth and bushy beard

*   *   *

Egnatius boasts white teeth, so very white
he smiles for ever puzzlingly polite.

The lawyer pleads amid a sobbing crowd:
he smiles. The widow wails, with sorrow bowed,
a widow who has lost her only son:
he smiles. Yes, everywhere, whatever's done,
he smiles. I call these gapes and grins misplaced,
a maudlin mania in the worst of taste.

Egnatius, listen. Though you claimed your home
in Sabine land, at Tiburs, or at Rome,
a fat Etruscan or gorged Umbrian,
or swarthy-faced and tusked Lanuvian,
a Past-the-Po (to near my native heath)
or any man who cleanly scours his teeth,
I still would hate you smiling daily dafter.
There's nothing sillier than silly laughter.

But you're a Spaniard. And the Spanish way
of cleaning teeth and ruddy gums, men say,
consists of urine-washes every day.
Thus, by your teeth's fresh sheen, our eyes may
    follow
how much of that foul brine you've had to
    swallow.

77. FUNNY

Martial

You're a pimp, you deal in slander,
you're an informer, forger, pander,
prizefighter-trainer too. It's funny,
Vacerra, that you have no money.

156

78. A DRIED-UP HARD-UP LECHER

Catullus

No slave or bug or moneybox,
spider or hearth – and yet you own
a father and stepmother known
for masticating nauseous rocks.

You lead a very happy life
with father and his wooden wife.
No wonder, for your health is fine,
digestion too. What's left to fear?
Not fires or falling masonry,
not poison-plot or thief's design.

From all life's dangers you're assured;
and then your body's grown as dry
as horn, or drier it may be,
with fasts, with heat and cold endured.
What health, what wealth these facts disclose.

No rheum comes dripping from your nose;
and what's more elegant, your rear,
like a salt-cellar polisht white,
won't function ten times in a year:
hard as a jewel or a bean,
the brightest object ever seen,
producing nothing, no, but clean.

Then keep a proper grateful sense
of such a blest convenience;
but all this borrowing I bar.
You're rich enough the way you are.

79. BRIBES OF BEAUTY

Seneca

W o u l d anyone credit that money changed hands during the trial of Clodius on a charge of secret adultery with Caesar's wife? Clodius, disguised as a girl, had violated the sacrificial rites that are said to be offered up on behalf of the People with all males rigorously excluded, driven outside the precinct, and with even the pictures of male creatures covered over.

Yet money was conveyed to the jurors; and worse even than such cash-bribery, lewderies were demanded of married women and wellborn youths as a sort of additional payment to secure the bargain. The charge thus involved far less criminality than the process of acquittal. For the man who was accused of a single adultery carried out his defence by spreading adulteries on all sides, and wasn't sure of his own skin till he had made the jurors as wickedly entangled as himself.

I shall cite Cicero's very words, because the facts are so bad as to be incredible. 'He arranged assignations and gave promises, he made pleas and gave gifts. Worse still – you good gods, what a pernicious state of things – on several of the jury, to round out their bribe, he even bestowed the enjoyment of various women and trysts with highborn youths.'

It's superfluous to hold up hands in horror at the cash-bribery. What was thrown-in was the really shocking thing. 'What about the wife of that prig of a chap would you fancy her? Right, that's fixed. Or the wife of that millionaire, you know who. You've only got to say the word and I'll get you the entry to her bed. If you don't get all the adultery you want, then give Clodius in as guilty. That lovely bit of stuff – that's what you hanker for? she's yours. No bother. She'll come along herself to visit you. I guarantee you a full night with the woman you point out, absolutely no slip-ups. My promise will be made good within the legal period of postponement.'

It means more to spread out such deeds than to commit them; it means the blackguarding of dignified matrons. These jurors had asked the Senate for a guard – a favour that would have been needed only by jurors who wished to convict Clodius. And their request was granted. Hence the witty query made by Catullus after the acquittal. He asked the jurors, 'Why did you request us for the guard? were you scared of having your money stolen from you?' And yet, amid jests of this sort, Clodius got away scotfree – a man who had been an adulterer before the trial, a pander during it, and whose method of avoiding punishment was far more criminal than the offence he was charged with.

More crime was committed than investigated. The question at issue was not whether one could be safe after a spot of adultery. What was proved was than one couldn't be safe without it.

80. AEMILIUS YOU'RE UNPLEASANT

Catullus

Aemilius, you're unpleasant, I can't tell
which end I'd choose for my offended nose.
The world's most vile, or least attractive smell:
I pick the nether aspect, I suppose.

It's toothless, while his two-inch tusks could bite,
with gums like trimmings of a shabby gig.
His slitted smile reminds you of the sight
when she-mules splash the summer. It's as big.

And yet this pleasant chap goes wenching still.
O strap him to the donkey's grinding-mill.
His sort of girl would think it a mere frolic
to kiss a rabid hangman panged with colic.

81. DINNER WITH THE
EMPEROR CALIGULA

Suetonius

THERE was scarcely any lady of note with whom he did not make free. His custom was to invite them with their husbands to dinner, and, as they passed by the couch on which he lay at table, to examine them closely all over, as men do when they are dealing in slaves. If one of them held down her face often from modesty, he forced it up with his hand. Afterwards, as often as he felt like it, he would leave the room, send for the woman who had most attracted his fancy, and in a short while come back with her, both of them rumpled and disordered. He would then make complimentary or disparaging comments on her performance in front of everyone, detailing the charms and defects of her person and the way she behaved alone with a man. To some wives he sent divorces in the names of their absent husbands and ordered them to be registered in the legal records.

82. THE GOD PRIAPUS
TELLS-OFF ADMIRERS

Anon.

No dried-up grapes could show such cracks.
Paler than boxwood or new wax,
she with her shanks and withered rump
makes pismire-ants seems hale and plump.

Her entrails gape, till with no knife
soothsayers can foretell her life:
sapless, so made of dirt and grit
that no one yet has seen her spit
and doctors think that she contains
ashes and sawdust in her veins.

Yet every night she comes and moans,
this amorous ghostly bag-of-bones.
Though to my hardy post I'm born,
I'm worn down by this funnel of horn.

*   *   *

You carrion-crow, you graveyard-crime,
you rotten remnant left by time,
you wet-nursed once in days decayed
Tithonus, Priam, Nestor – that's
unless when they were puling brats
you were a crone. 'A man!' you pray.
You hope afresh to turn a maid –
all things are possible, if you pay.

[*Priapus was represented as a herm (a head on a stock of wood) together with phallus. Tithonus, etc., were proverbially long-living heroes far in the mythical past.*]

83. LOVING ABUSE

Catullus

Lesbia insults me while her husband's by,
The fool is pleased and never wonders why.
You ass, you're blind. If she could let me be,
then she'd be whole; but while she curses me,
I'm sticking in her thought, and more, she feels
a pricking hate – and so, on heat, she squeals.

*   *   *

How could I blacken her, my only good?
She's dearer than my eyes: how could I hate?
I couldn't. I'd stop loving if I could –
but you and Tappo must exaggerate. . .

*   *   *

Still Lesbia goes the rounds abusing me.
Death take me, but she wants me still as lover.
How's that? I too abuse her endlessly,
and death may take me if I do not love her.

84. BRAWL

Propertius

She'd tricked and cheated me so much, I swore
to shift my bed and even up the score.

Phyllis near Dian on the Aventine
bores me when sober. Drunk, she's different stuff.
And Teia from Tarpeia's Grove, when wine
has warmed her charm, no single man's enough.

I thought I'd call them in and soothe the night.
I'd try a change of kisses. Yes, I'd dare.
A single couch in soft and shadowy light –
how were we placed? I stretched between the pair.

From summer-cups of glass my Lygdamus
poured the rich wines matured on Lesbian ground.
Nile sent the piper. Phyllis danced for us
with castanets, with roses scattering round.

The dwarf with gnarling fingers played to me,
his stubby fingers twirled the flute unheeded.
The well-filled lamps were blinking drowsily,
the table squatly on its legs receded.

I diced. Then loud the dicing-boxes rang,
the Dog and not the Venus still was thrown.
They bared their breasts, unwatched. Unheard, they
    sang.
At the Lanuvian Gates I stood, alone.

The hinges grated suddenly outside.
I heard a murmuring voice invade my lair.
O, Cynthia flung the panels open wide,
lovely with wrath, with wild and lovely hair.

My wine-loose lips went pallid and I aged.
Down from my fingers fell the cup and cracked.
She flamed and all the woman in her raged.
I thought I saw a city being sacked.

She scratched at Phyllis' face and made her weep
while Teia shouted out, 'Help, fire and murder!'
The scurrying lights awoke the square from sleep.
Madly she screamed: for streets the people heard her.

The girls, with tresses torn, crept disarrayed
to find the nearest pub with shuttered door.
Cynthia stood glorying in the wreck she'd made,
then came and slapt my wicked face once more.

My throat she branded, biting till I bled,
but chiefly at my sinful eyes she aimed;
and when she tired of beating at my head,
she lugged out Lygdamus who lay ashamed

beneath the couch. In vain he clasped my knees.
Poor slave, I too was humbled in defeat.
I raised my palms. At last she heard my pleas,
although she scarcely let me touch her feet.

She said, 'If truly now for peace you've prayed,
you'll follow out the laws that I declare.
You must not lounge in Pompey's Colonnade
or watch the shows that crowd the horrid square,

cricking your neck to see the upper-row,
or lift a litter's hangings for a word.
But Lygdamus, the cause of all, must go.
Shackle his legs and sell him. Have you heard?'

I answered, 'Yes, my dear, the lesson's learned.'
She smiled to see me grown so well behaved.
Then everywhere the girls had touched, she burned
some sulphur, and the doors she cleansed and laved.

'Bring us new lamps with different oil,' she bade.
She sprinkled sulphur thrice upon my head.
She called for change of sheets, and fresh were laid.
We ventured on a second marriage-bed.

85. DECEIVED

Ovid

Cupid, be off and leave me, quiver and all.
No passion's worth it, when it makes us want to die.
And still I want to die, whenever I remember
the things you did to me.
You're lovely, but born to cause me an endless heart-
   ache.
It wasn't half-erased tablets that gave you away,
it wasn't presents arriving behind my back.
I only wish the evidence was circumstantial
so that you'd loudly deny the charges
and I'd believe you in the end.
Why is my case so damnably watertight?
Happy the man who may defend his girl's devotion
without the quiver of an eyelid,
the man to whom his girl may simply say,
'But I've done nothing.'
And hard of heart is he, a fool is he,
who wants to aggravate his own despair,
who gains a scratched and bleeding victory
by proving that he's miserable.

I, to my sorrow, perfectly sober,
with wine upon the table, was myself the witness
of your wantonness.
You thought I was asleep.
I saw the pair of you exchanging various comments
by movements of the eyebrows,
and all your nods were volubly expressive.

Your eyes too had a lot to say,
the table with its wine-scribbles,
and fingers nimbly eloquent.
I understood the discourse of your silence,
your words as well, which had their double meanings,
prearranged signs and glances of collusion.

And now the tables were taken away
and almost all the guests departed.
Only a couple of lads, dead drunk, lay flat.
Then you'd the courage to start ardent kisses,
the pair of you, and you, my girl, weren't lacking
in enterprise. The way you kissed and kissed
didn't at all suggest a sister primly
kissing her brother. A voluptuous mistress
warmly engufing her impetuous lover
was what I saw, the way you leaned and lifted.

'What's going on?' I cried at last.
'Where are taking those raptures?
They're mine. What's mine, I'll claim.
These things you're doing are done by me and you,
or you and me, but not by a third person.'

I said all that, and a lot more as well,
which misery put in my mouth. And as for her,
she blushed, she certainly blushed, she blushed as red
as the reddest dawn or a bride who slides away
her fame-hued veil and stands in her husband's eyes,
as red as roses burning among the lilies,
as red as Assyrian ivory stained by Lydian girls
to give it a mellow tone with age.
That's how she looked. At least, like some of those
    things:
I fear I overdid the similes.

At any rate it's true she never loo[k]
as lovely as then.
She cast her eyes upon the floor
and downcast eyes were just the
   charming.
She had a melancholy touch,
and grief was just the thing to ma[k]

I'd meant to tear her hair and spo[il]
she'd never had her hair done be[fore]
and give her tender cheeks some p[ink]
But when I saw her face, my ar[m]
   nerved.
She had her weapons to repel atta[ck]
I, who a moment before had been
now as a suppliant, of my own acc[ord]
begged her to give me kisses as g[ood as]
   given.
She smiled and gave me her best a[nd]
A kiss that would have snatched fr[om Jove]
his threepronged bolts.
And now I was anguished lest the
had had as good a kiss.
I only hope she gave him kisses less
less variously absorbing, an inferior

The kiss she granted me forgivingl[y]
was a far better kiss than those I'd
I had the impression she'd learned
Yes, that remarkable kiss was an om[en]
I'm worried that she joined her li[ps]
and mine to hers, with such a lovi[ng]
And yet that worry's not the only on[e]
I don't complain that kisses were ex[cellent]
(although I do complain of that as w[ell]

169

d

ɪng to make her

her charming.

her toilet –
er –
ʊper smacks.
s were quite un-

.
lemented,
ʼd
ʼd as those she'd

heartiest kiss.
n God Almighty

her fellow

omplete,
rand.

ught her.
mething new.
ʊous sign.
to mine,
deftness.
.
langed
ll),

ɛd to meet.
l for giving

on the roof
Of course he
kissing each

uld spot who.
t long for the

E. Hey, I says,
ɔf? Chasing a

for a beastly
s she still in?

o across to our
Then everyone
the other place.
ffair to end in
of the Cross.
s else?
e absolutely sure
of women. She
d training.

Pal. So she can convince the man who saw her that he didn't see her, see? No matter if he saw her wide-open at the game a hundred times, she must deny it point-blank, with the utmost innocence.

(Sings.)

She's cheeky, the sly wench,
she's glib and she won't blench
at telling any tales at all, without a single blink.
She's crooked and she's fly,
and any tricks she'll try,
for she's as shrewd as skirts are made, and braver than
you think.

If anyone accuses her,
says how her lover uses her,
you'll find at once the tart she is, and her unshaken
nerve.
No matter how found-out she is,
you'll see without a doubt she is
the purest girl that ever was; for any lie will serve.

She's plausible and skilful,
as ready as she's wilful,
she'll swear the nose from off your face and you will
ask her pardon.
O once she starts her smiling,
her wheedling and beguiling,
you'd better say your prayers because she'll lead you
up the garden.

The devil's in her sighing.
She never need go buying
at costermonger's stalls or shops the apples she re-
quires.

She's stocked with garden-stuff
and sauces too, enough
for dishing up all devilries to safeguard her desires.

Perip. Well, I'll take your message in, if she's still there.

87. HOPELESS LOVER

Laberius

I fell into love like a cockroach into a basin.

88. TWO REQUESTS

Propertius

O you who are beautiful, you who were born
to hurt me, to be loved, to be beautiful,
O you alone born to be all these things, please
let me come and see you more often.

My poetry shall make your beauty famous
more than any other in the whole world.
Please, Calvus and Catullus, have mercy and let me
write even better poems than you did.

89. SONG AND LOVE

Tuccianus

Song begets love,
      love begets song.
            We cannot break the ring
            Then let us sing,
      that we may love
and love that we may sing.

90. DON'T MARRY

Plautus

[*Pleusicles has won over the trusted slave of the man who has the girl he wants. The slave has worked out a scheme which involves the co-operation of an old gentleman; and he and Pleusicles set about flattering the latter.*]

Pleusicles (to the slave). Well, I must say you're a chap after my own heart.

Slave. Very good to hear you say it, sir. Cheers me up no end.

Old Gentleman. He says no more than you deserve, lad.

Pleu. (to Old Gentleman). But I'm really ashamed of myself, my dear sir, I really am wretched about it all. It's getting me down. Body and soul, I'm in a bad way.

O.G. Ashamed, wretched, down flat? what's the trouble?

Pleu. Just think of it. Here I am putting on to you, a man well on in life, all these stupid young miseries of mine, not the sort of thing for a man of your respected character. Asking you to come out strong on my behalf and get me out of the mess I've got myself into – this love-affair of mine. Respectable men of your age don't like getting mixed up in such dubious matters. I feel simply awful at dumping my bag of troubles on your back in your old age.

Slave. Well, sir, you're a new sort of lover, you are, the first known in this odd world of ours, if you're actually ashamed of anything you do. No, no, sir, you're not in love, you only think you are, you're only a wisp of a shadow of a lover, not the life-size thing.

Pleu. All the same, to go bothering him at his age with my love-troubles?

O.G. What are you talking about? Not very polite, are you? You take me for a regular old death's-head, eh? Cheating my coffin, is that what you're trying to infer? keeping on living when I ought to fold my hands and ask to be laid out? Just take another look at me, my dear boy. I'm not a day over fifty-four – still as keen of sight, quick of hand, and nimble of foot as I ever was.

Slave. His hair may be white, sir, but there's not a streak of grey in his spirit. He's just the same lively person he was on his first birthday.

Pleu. That's an absolute fact, lad, and what am I doing but proving it? Why, look how friendly and good-natured he is – couldn't be younger.

O.G. All right, my dear boy, go ahead. The more you ask of me, the more I'll show you how much good will I feel towards you in this little trouble of yours.

Pleu. I don't need to be shown. I'm quite convinced already.

O.G. All the same, I want you to convince yourself by experience, not just at second-hand. *(Knowingly.)* Unless a man has been in love himself and gone through the whole bag of tricks, he can hardly see inside a lover's heart. But speaking for myself, I can say I've still got a trifle of warmth – yes, still fresh and alive-o – here in this carcass of mine. I'm not yet dried up and unable to get a kick out of all the things that charm a man and tickle him well up. You'll find I can still crack a good joke and I'm a proper sort of tactful guest for your dinner-parties – not the sort of person who contradicts everyone. Lack of table-tact is the one thing I really watch myself out for. I believe in taking a fair share in the conversation of course, and a fair share of holding my tongue too when someone else is holding forth. I'm not one of those fellows who keep on spitting and hawking and sniffling and blowing their nose all the while. I give you my word. I was born in a refined town, not in the uncouth country-side, a lump of a clumping bumpkin only used to frumps, dumps, stumps, and grumps.

Slave. Now, sir, did you ever meet a more delightful old gent in all your born life, if he lives up to half what he says. Anyone with half an eye can see he's been brought up in a real cultured environment, with a tip-top education.

O.G. (pleased). And what's more, you'll find me better at showing what a proper brought-up person I am, than at talking about it. Why, at a party you'll never see me pulling another guest's girl down on the floor, and I don't sneak the titbits when no one's looking, and I don't take more cups out of the punch-bowl than I ought to in my turn, and I don't start a brawl when I've had a drop too much, no, I never do. If there's someone there who gets on my nerves, I just turn my back in the middle of the conversation and stalk off home. When I'm at table, I'm a thousand per cent. for being gracious, glad-some, and gratuitous.

Slave. Lord, sir, nobody could help being all smiles with you about. Just show me three such men in all the world, and I'll give you their weight in gold for them, yes.

Pleu. No, lad, you're going too far. You won't find his equal. Not a man of his age that's such a pleasant friend – nor so trusty and helpful. No, lad.

O.G. Before I've done, I'll make you admit I'm still a young fellow like yourself in all my ways and you couldn't have asked anyone who'd better help you out of your fix. Do you need a sort of legal adviser – you know, glowering, shouting at the top of his voice? That's me. Just look now. *(He glowers.)* Or someone all soft-and-soothing syrup? You'll say I'm milder than the sea when it's a duck-pond, and gentler than a caressing zephyr of the spring. Just look now. *(He grins.)* And out of this selfsame material *(he taps his chest)* I'll produce you any character you want – the gayest of gay dinner-guests or the perfect buffoon of the party, or the most slap-up caterer you could ask for. While as for dancing, there's no ballet pro that can do a bit of pirouetting or a really seductive cancan like I can when I'm in the mood.

Slave. With such a bunch of high-class talents, sir, you couldn't choose anyone more suited, you just couldn't. What more do you want?

Pleu. I want the power to repay such a devotion to my poor little cause – yours too, lad. I appreciate the hard work you're putting in. *(To Old Gentleman.)* But I'm worried about the expense I'm drawing you into.

O.G. *(slapping him on shoulder).* You're a donkey. Now if you spend even a penny on a wicked wife or a bad friend, that's waste, that's expense. But money spent on a good guest and a genuine friend is money to be entered on the credit side – just as no man counts as a loss what he gives to the gods. Thank the Lord I've got enough to entertain you fairly well at my home. Eat, drink, do just as you please in my company, and enjoy yourself all you can. It's Liberty Hall here and I let myself go freely as well. I like to live my own life. I'm pleased I can say I'm a rich man. If I'd wanted it, I could have married a proper lady with a solid estate. But it wasn't my idea to open the door to a yapping bitch.

Slave. But why not? After all, it's a delightful duty to set about getting children.

O.G. Getting a free life is more delightful in my view.

Slave. I see that you're a man who can give good advice to himself as well as to someone else.

O.G. Yes, yes, it's all very pleasant to marry a good wife – if there happened to be any place on earth that bred such unusual creatures. But am I to bring home a a woman who'd never once say to me, 'Husband mine, do please buy me some wool so I can make a soft warm overcoat for you, and some nice heavy suits of clothes, to be sure you won't be cold this winter.' You'd never hear a wife talking like that. O no, before the rooster has stopped crowing, she'd be nudging me awake and nagging at me. 'Husband mine, give me some money so I can make my mother a present on Mother's Day. Give me some money so I can make preserves. Give me some money so I can cross the palm of the fortune-teller at Minerva's Festival – and the dream-interpreter, and the crystal-gazer, and the star-reader. Besides, it's all wrong if I don't send a fee along to that clever woman who tells the future from your eyebrows. And there's the dress-maker, I must give her a tip, or I won't be able to look anyone in the face. Not to mention the catering woman, she's in an awful temper with me. And the midwife, she was ever so rude about the small sum I sent her. O dear me, you don't mean to say you'll send nothing, not a brass farthing, to the nurse who looks after the slaves born under your own roof?' All that ruinous chucking-away of money – and I only said a fraction of it – that's what stops me from getting a wife who'll drive me dotty with such gabble.

Slave. The gods are kind to you, sir . . . But now listen to what I have to suggest – the job we've got on hand. I've thought up a splendid trick for getting my long-haired master on the run and giving our friend here a chance to carry off the girl he's got shut up all for himself.

O.G. Out with it.

Slave. First let me have that signet ring of yours.

O.G. What use is it to you?

Slave. Let me have it and I'll explain.

O.G. Here you are then.

Slave. Then here's the scheme to get him out of the way. Listen. *(He pauses.)*

Pleu. We're both listening like mad.

Slave. My master, you see, is the world's most absorbed woman-chaser – in the past, present, or future.

Pleu. It's a fact.

Slave. He considers himself a handsomer fellow than Alexander the Conquering Hero, and he's never tired of telling how all the women in the town insist on hanging about his neck.

O.G. There's many a husband who wishes the dog was really so magnetically attractive. I know him. I know all about him. So come to the point.

Slave. Can you turn up some gorgeous-looking piece, sir, with a naughty sort of resourceful mind?

O.G. (considering). Freeborn or freedwoman?

Slave. Doesn't matter in the least. Just hand me a wench whose one aim in life is quite simply hard cash, whose body earns her what she needs bodily, and whose wits are as crafty as they're made. I said wits not brains, for it's my considered opinion that no woman has the latter commodity.

O.G. A swell piece, eh? Or one that hasn't yet started swelling?

Slave. O you know the sort of thing – as full of sap as she can be without bursting, and the younger the better.

O.G. I've got the very thing. One of the family dependants. A magnificent tart, and yet only just started laying herself out to the best advantage.

Slave. Now get it clear. Ask her along to your house at once. Then fetch her here, all got up like a married woman, with a respectable hat and her hair done up on top of her head, in ribbons. She's to be your wife. I mean, that's what she is to say of herself.

Pleu. I don't get the drift of all this.

Slave. You will. *(To the Old Gentleman.)* Has she got a maid?

O.G. Yes, and a sly-puss too.

Slave (peremptorily). Good, we want her too. Give the tart and the tartlet the following instructions. The mistress is to pretend she's your wife, turning up her toes with longing for my master, and she's to give this ring of yours to sly-puss, and the sly-puss is to hand it over to me as the go-between.

O.G. No need to talk so loud. I'm not deaf. I have the full use of my ears.

Slave (more quietly). I'll give my master the ring and say it comes from your wife as a token that I'm to lead him along to a tryst with her. He'll fall into the thing head first, sir. That's the sort he is. He'll be crazy to grab her, sir. He's only got room for one idea in that head of his, and it's bedwork.

O.G. Well, if you got the Sun in heaven himself to do the job of looking round for a pair of delectable girls expressly made for this kind of thing, you couldn't do better. Put your mind at rest.

Slave. Spring to it, sir. We need them quick. *(Old Gentleman goes out).* And now, Pleusicles, I'll tell you how to smuggle your lady-love out while my master's on the rampage.

91. GONE

Propertius

The girl I loved has left me. She has left me.

Do you tell me, friend, I have no cause for distress?
There are no enemies save those we love . . .
Kill me and my anger would be less.
O can I see her leaning on another,
who was mine, who was mine, so lately?
Then I would say 'You are mine' to her aloud . . .
But love's king of yesterday becomes by fate
tomorrow's fool. That is the way of love.
Great kings have lain in the dust, very great lords;
there was an old city called Thebes,
and Troy had towers once.
Think of the gifts I gave and the songs I made.
Yet all that time I had her, she would never say the
    words
'I love you.'

92. A LETTER TO A
CHAPERONING EUNUCH

Ovid

BAGOUS, you are the one whose duty it is to keep watch
over your mistress. Please listen to what I have to say, it
won't take long.

Yesterday morning I saw a young lady walking in the
Portico that holds the statues of the wicked daughters
of Danaus. I liked the look of her, and at once wrote her
a note with my request. With trembling hand she
scribbled back, 'I can't.' And when I asked why she
couldn't, she told me the reason. Your surveillance,
she said, is too strict.

Now, keeper, if you're sensible — take my word for it —
give up deserving my ill will. Everybody wants to see
the end of someone that they fear. Besides, her husband
isn't in his right mind. Whoever would take such a lot
of trouble to guard something which is never dimin-
ished or lost, even if you take no care of it all? Still, if
he's mad, let him indulge his madness. Let him still believe that the object which gives universal pleasure is
chastely all his own. By your favour, she may in secret
gain her freedom — so that one day you may receive the
gift you've given. Are you prepared to be a confidant?
Then the mistress becomes obedient to the slave. But
if you fear to be an accomplice, all you have to do is
close your eyes. You notice that she's reading a letter all
by herself. Well, why not suppose that her mother sent
it? Does a stranger come sidling up? There's no reason
why you shouldn't recognize an old acquaintance. What

if your mistress goes to visit a sick girl friend, who doesn't happen to be sick? You can still be of opinion that the friend is sick as can be. If she spends an extremely long time inside the temple at the sacrifice, you needn't complain that the waiting aggravated you. Just let your head hang down on your chest and give yourself up to snoring. And don't go inquiring as to what sort of thing can happen inside the temple of Isis in her pure linen drape. Nor be in the least afraid of the theatres with their rounded lines of seats.

An accomplice in the intrigue will gain inexhaustible gratitude; and after all what is less trouble than just to hold one's tongue? The slave who shares his lady's secret has everything his own way, he can turn the house upside down and he feels no stripes. He's the lord of all he sees, and the rest, a scrubby lot, are mere grovellers. To cover up the facts, he invents a new set; and what the mistress sets her seal of approval on, the master tamely underwrites. Let the latter contract his brow and summon up all his wrinkles: the wife knows a caress or two that makes him end up by eating out of her hand. All the same, it's up to her to impute some rigours and faults to you now and then, to squeeze out a shower of tears and call you a curse, a harsh jailer. While you on your part trump up some charge which she can easily explain away to her credit. Use fake accusations to blur out the least hint of the truth. And you'll see your privileges and your slave's income steadily increase – and before you know where you are, you'll be a free man.

You see the chains clanking round the necks of informers. The stinking jail receives the hearts that don't deserve to be believed. Water, water everywhere, says Tantalus and not a drop to drink, and he snatches at the apples as they bob out of his reach. He talked too much, that man. You know the tale about Juno. While the keeper she set was watching Io too strictly, he died before his time; but as for the naughty girl, she became a goddess.

I've seen fetters on the bruised legs of a man who told a husband about his wife's goings-on. He got less than his deserts, I say. An unruly tongue did nothing but hurt two people. It grieved the husband and it wrecked the wife's reputation. Trust me. No husband is pleased to hear the truth about his wife. Even if he avidly listens, he isn't happy at the tidings. If he's indifferent, you're wasting your precious information on ears that don't give a damn for it; and if he's really in love, then he's cast into despair by your officiousness.

Remember too, a slip, even when divulged, isn't so easy to prove. She comes up for trial before a judge whose prejudices all work on her side. Why, even if he saw the deed with his own eyes, he'll begin to believe her as she persists in denying. In the end he'll give the verdict against his own eyes and force himself to accept it. Let him only see his dear wife weeping and he will shed a few tears himself. Then he'll say, 'That fool who can't hold his tongue must be punished.' Don't you see how unequal is the contest on which you've embarked? If you lose, the whip will whistle over you, while she sleeps calmly in the bosom of the judge.

It's not as if we're meditating crimes. We're not meeting to mix poisons. My hand isn't gleaming with a drawn sword. We merely ask your permission to let us make love in safety. Now what could be more harmless than such a petition?

93. IN DEFENCE OF THE ROMAN POETS

Aulus Gellius

A YOUNG middle-class man from the land of Asia, gifted and well-off in manners and fortune, with a taste and talent for music, was giving a birthday party to his friends and teachers in a little country place near the city of Athens. We were accompanied to the festivities by the rhetorician Antonius Julianus, a public teacher of young men, who spoke with a Spanish accent, but was quite eloquent as well as deeply read in our early literature. When we had all finished eating and drinking, and the time came for conversation, Julianus asked for the singers and lyre-players to be brought in, the most skilful of both sexes, whom he knew that our host had at hand.

So the boys and girls were brought in and they sang most delightfully several odes of Anacreon and Sappho, as well as some love-elegies by more recent poets, which were full of charm and grace. But we were particularly entertained by some very attractive verses of Anacreon, composed in his old age, which I noted down so that at times the labour and worry of this literary task of mine might now and then be relieved by the sweetness of poetical tones:

> Forge-god, as you shape the silver,
> hammer out for me no weapons.
> I've no use for clang of battle.
> Rather make a cup for drinking

deep as ever you can make it.
Carve on it no stars or wagons –
what care I for things like Pleiads,
all the star-folk like Boötes?
Make me vines with clusters hanging,
let the Lovegod and my Darling
show in gold, both busy treading
grapes, and with them show the Wine-god.

Then several Greeks who were among the guests, men
of refinement, who did not lack a large acquaintance
with our literature, began to attack and harass Julianus
as an uncouth bumpkin, since he was sprung from the
land of Spain, was a mere ranter of raucous and screech-
ing speech, and taught exercises in a language devoid of
the lures and rewarding loveliness of Venus and the
Muse. They demanded more than once his opinion of
Anacreon and other poets of the same sort.

'Now, have any of your poets ever written such melli-
fluous and captivating poems – except perhaps Catullus
in a few poems and Calvus in a few more. Laevius is
involved and obscure. Hortensius without charm, Memmius unpolished, and in brief all your poets are lacking
in fineness and harmony.'

Julianus, moved to anger and indignation, spoke out
in defence of his mother-tongue as if he were defending
his altars and home-fires. 'I am ready enough to grant
you that in lewdery and dirt you are fabulously the first,
and that, just as you surpass us in your enjoyment of
clothes and food, so you also do it in the debauchery of
your songs. But don't be in such a hurry to write us of
the Latin race off as ignorant of all Venus charm, a set
of gawping savages. Allow me, I beg you, to cover up my
head with my cloak – as they say Socrates did when
making a smutty remark – and I'll show you that our

forefathers also were lovers and devotees of Venus long
before the poets you have mentioned.'

Then, lying back with his head veiled, he chanted in
the smoothest of tones some lines by Valerius Aedituus,
an early poet, and others by Porcius Licinius and Q.
Catullus; and I'm sure that nothing neater, more elegant,
polished, and terse can be cited in either Latin or Greek:

The lines by Aedituus ran thus:

> When, Pamphila, I try to tell you
> the innermost of my heart,
> what shall I ask of you?
> Words die upon my lips.
> A sudden sweat
> drips from my burning breast.
> Silent with love, I ask you nothing
> accepting death.

And he added some more verses by the same poet, no
less appealing:

> Phileros, why the torch?
> We've got no need of it.
> Let's go the way we are,
> with hearts aflame.
> No gust of the wild wind
> can put out such a blaze,
> no torrent of rain falling
> sheer from the skies.
> No one but Venus knows the way to quench
> the fire she starts.
> No other force can wield
> so stark a power.

He also recited the following lines by Porcius Licinius:

> Shepherds of the lambs
> still small from the wombs of the ewes,
> is it fire you're after?
> Come over here. Here's what you seek.
> For man is fire.
> If with my fingertip I touch the wood,
> it blazes up.
> Your flock's aflame. All I behold is fire.

The lines from Q. Catullus were these:

> My soul has left me.
> Surely it's fled away to Theotimus.
> He is its refuge.
> What then if I should beg him to refuse
> to let the runaway in – to shut it out.
> I'll go to him.
> But what if I myself am caught and held?
> What shall I do?
> Venus, come and aid me.

94. THE MARRIAGE OF THE EMPEROR HONORIUS

(a) Claudian

Mingle your breaths and warm into love, you pair,
the newborn truth that henceforth your breasts will
   share.
O let your twining fingers express your vows
as close as ivy on flowering chestnut-boughs,
as close as vines embracing a poplar-tree.

And let your kisses, given and taken, be
softer than those of the doves with their plaintive cry–
and learn, as soul meets soul on your lips, to lie
while the hands of sleep are soothing your panting
   frames.

O warm the purple sheet with your royal games,
bravely ennoble with richer and virgin red
the coverlets Tyrian-dyed on your marriage-bed.
Then leap from the wetted sheets in victor-delight
showing the wounds of the battle of love-by-night.

Through all the hours of the dark let flutes resound
and the crowd indulge in their jests, no longer bound
by the rigorous law. Ho, sport with your officers now.
soldiers, wherever you are, as the rules allow.

Sport with the lady, you girls, wherever you are.
For this is the voice that echoes from star to star:
over the peoples, over the seas, it has cried:
Handsome Honorius takes Maria as bride.

All the while Giton stood laughing by, helpless with merriment. Quartilla noticed him and asked with extreme interest whose lad he was. 'Mine,' I said.

'Then why hasn't he kissed me?' she remarked. She called him over and set herself busily to kissing him. Soon her hand went straying. 'What's this?' she said. 'Tomorrow it'll do well enough as a whet for my larger appetite. Today I don't want any common-and-garden fare after trying out a rare dainty.'

As she said this, Psyche went up to her with a laugh and whispered in her ear something I couldn't hear. 'Yes, yes,' Quartilla replied, 'a splendid idea. There'll never be a prettier occasion for our Pannychis to find out what it means to be a woman.'

Without delay they brought in a rather lovely little girl, who didn't look more than seven years of age, the very one who had attended on Quartilla in the visit to our inn. The whole company applauded and demanded an immediate marriage. The ceremony began despite my amazement, my protests that Giton was a most modest and innocent boy, incapable of playing a part in such a wanton performance, and that the girl was far too young to endure the routine of a bride.

'Why,' said Quartilla, 'is she any younger than I was when I first went through it? May my Juno turn on me if I can remember at all when I was a maid. When I was a child, I had my games with boys of the same age, and when I grew bigger I used to romp with bigger boys, and so on, stage by stage, till I've come to where I am today. And that's how the proverb arose, I'm sure, that she who bore the calf will bear the bull.'

And so, to ensure that Giton did not encounter any worse hazard in my absence, I rose to assist in the details of the wedding. Psyche had already wrapped the girl's head in the nuptial flame-coloured veil, and the low comedian led the way with a torch. A long trail of drunken women followed, clapping their hands after strewing the marriage-bed with its unhallowed coverlet. Then Quartilla, kindled by the lewd tones of the revellers, with her own hands caught hold of Giton and dragged him into the room. Not indeed that the boy showed any reluctance or the girl seemed at all averse to the idea of matrimony.

When they were abed with the doors closed, we settled down on the threshold of the room; and first of all Quartilla clapped an eager eye to a slit made naughtily on purpose, and watched their childish play with lascivious enjoyment. She also drew me with a gentle hand to share in the spectacle; and as our faces met warmly against the slit, every now and then she tore herself away from the peepshow and with her vehement and lax mouth she harassed me with a sort of stealthy kisses.

(c) Statius

May merciful Cynthia hasten the tenth month of birth,
but you, Lucina, spare her. And baby, you,
spare your mother, don't hurt her tender womb,
her swollen breasts. When Nature in secrecy marks
your features, draw much beauty from your father,
but from your mother yet more.

95. TO A RING

Ovid

O Ring, about to encircle my darling's finger,
there's nothing valuable in you
except the giver's love.
Go as a pleasing gift.
I hope she smiles, receiving you,
and slides you at once upon her outstretched finger.
Be sure to serve her well while she is faithful,
nicely fit her, enclosing
her finger in your easy circle.
O happy Ring, she'll play about with you,
and I, poor fellow,
now envy my own presents.

O, if only
I suddenly could be changed and become this ring
by Circe's arts or those
of the old man who shifted shape to shape.
Then I would pray for you to touch her breast,
I'd pray for her to insert
her left hand underneath her dress.
However light, however good a fit,
off her finger I'd slip by some contrivance
and fall within her bosom.
And when she used me to seal her secret tablets,
to ensure her seal was neither dry nor sticky
and wouldn't catch in the wax,
she'd lift me to her lips and moisten me.
But I'd refuse to seal a note

which summoned someone to my grief.
And should she hand me over to be stored
inside her chest-of-drawers, I wouldn't go,
I'd narrow my circle and I'd grip her finger.

Listen, my girl, I'd never be a nuisance,
a burden distressing to your slender finger.
Wear me when bathing in warm water
and accept the inconvenience –
the water getting underneath the stone –
but O, I fear that when I saw you naked
I couldn't control myself a moment longer.
Ring as I was, I'd somehow enact the lover.
Yet why start sighing for what's impossible?
Go, little gift.
Let her understand that what I send with you
is my devotion.

96. MARRIAGE SONG

Catullus

You haunt the Muses Hill,
Urania's son. It's you
that bids the bride lie still
    O Hymenaeus Hymen
    O Hymen Hymenaeus.

Garland your sacred head
with marjoram, and spread
the long flame-coloured veil;
on your feet small and pale
buckle the yellow shoe.

Here's holiday. Awake,
sing the gay songs of love,
sing them out silverly,
leap on the earth and shake
the pine torch out above.

For now shall Vinia wed
with Manlius, as fair
as Venus when she stood
on Ida: save that she
and all she brings is good.

As flourishing in hue
as a thick myrtle-spray
which Dryads every day
feed with their gleaming dew,
their playmate and their care.

Call her within the gate:
she longs for her new mate.
Bind love about her heart
as ivy curls its flowers
around a sturdy tree.

Come, maidens, do your part.
The day soon comes for you.
Then chant triumphantly
    O Hymenaeus Hymen
    O Hymen Hymenaeus.

Cry and the god will hear
and he will know our need
and soon we'll find him near
because he loves to lead
two hearts whose love is true.

What lovers' god could be
invoked more worthily?
what god could be more kind?
    O Hymenaeus Hymen
    O Hymen Hymenaeus.

The father calls you here,
sighing. The maiden breaks
her zone for you abed.
For you the bridegroom wakes,
listening for every tread.

The blossom-maid you snatch
out of her mother's breast
for a young man to wed.
    O Hymenaeus Hymen
    O Hymen Hymenaeus.

Venus would lose her best,
the joys that peace could give,
unless you deigned to nod.
What god is there to match
himself against this god?

Spread wide each golden door.
She comes, the torches shake
bright tresses in her wake.
True modesty is slow.
She weeps that she must go.

You're safe now, weep no more,
Aurunculeia. Lo,
never a lovelier one
has stood to face the sun
bright from the ocean shore.

Thus in the chequered grass
a rich man's garden-pride
the hyacinth might sway.
But come, make no delay,
come forth, you lagging bride.

Yes, bride, the moments pass.
Please hear the words we've cried.
See how the torches make
gold tresses where they shake.
Come forth at length O bride.

Your husband will not cast
lightly your love away
to wanton girls at last
nor ever wish to rest
save on your softer breast,

but as the supple vine
that clings about the bough
into your limbs he'll twine
forever. While there's a day,
come, bride, fulfil your vow.

What joys approach for him,
noon may not make them dim
nor midnight see them fail.
But come, make no delay,
come forth, you lagging bride.

Boys, wave the torches now.
I see the bridal veil.
Cry out on every side:
> *O Hymenaeus Hymen*
> *O Hymen Hymenaeus.*

Let merriment be stirred,
traditional jests be said.
Let the lad scatter nuts
since now at last he's heard
the bridegroom leaves his bed.

My lad, give nuts away.
You've met your match today.
Enough with nuts you've played.
Marriage-law is obeyed.
Give nuts, my lad, give nuts.

You long turned up your nose
at girls as worthless sluts
and now the barber shaves
your cheeks. Bewail your woes
and scatter nuts for slaves.

And, man, though folk deride,
'He'll soon be back again,'
be faithful and abstain.
> *O Hymen Hymenaeus*
> *O Hymenaeus Hymen.*

Licensed was all that play,
but be no longer weak.
A husband's different.
> *O Hymen Hymenaeus*
> *O Hymenaeus Hymen.*

And so I bid you, bride,
be kind or he will seek
elsewhere what you've denied.
> *O Hymen Hymenaeus*
> *O Hymenaeus Hymen.*

Well-omened then and wise,
lift your gold feet once more,
enter the polisht door.
> *O Hymenaeus Hymen*
> *O Hymen Hymenaeus.*

How eagerly he lies
where wide the purple's spread,
his soul to you he sighs.
> *O Hymenaeus Hymen*
> *O Hymen Hymenaeus.*

As warm as you he glows
from burning foot to head,
and deeper love he knows.
> *O Hymenaeus Hymen*
> *O Hymen Hymenaeus.*

Quick, quick, young lad, set free
her rounded arm. You see,
there is the husband's bed.
  O Hymenaeus Hymen
  O Hymen Hymenaeus.

You reverend matrons wedded
to ancient husbands, place
her right for the embrace.
  O Hymenaeus Hymen
  O Hymen Hymenaeus.

Bridegroom, your wife is bedded.
Her gleaming flowerface
is glancing at the door
like a pale poppy or
a daisy roundly white.

By heaven, I declare,
you make as fine a sight
and Venus loves you too.
Come, there is little day,
enter, make no delay.

Not long have you delayed.
Now Venus be your aid
since frankly you unbare
your love for all to view
because your love is true.

Let him first count the dust
of Africa, and count
the stars burnt overhead
who hopes to sum the joy
and ardour of this bed.

Yes, let the kisses mount.
The house desires a boy.
Such stock should know no gap,
but procreate they must
within a worthy lap.

I long myself to see
a small Torquatus raise
his hands up with a smile
towards his father while
he clasps his mother's knee.

And may the gazers trace
his father in his face,
for thus their happy eyes
will also recognize
her womb's fidelity.

And may her honour's praise
as worthily descend
as once that paragon
faithful Penelope
lent honour to her son.

Now, maidens, shut the door.
Enough of jests, no more.
Hold to your wedded truth,
you loving pair, and spend
in joy your vigorous youth.

[*Though based on Greek lyric and hymnal forms, this epithalamion for the poet's friend Manlius Torquatus and Vinia Aurunculeia is essentially Roman. Note that it is not a poem about a marriage, but a dramatically conceived song to be sung at the marriage, dealing with each stage of the processional rite, and ending with the moment of consummation.*]

97. THE SLAVE ANSWERS HIS MASTER
Horace

You're for adultery; for brothels, I.
Shall either man upon the cross then die?
At need, in open lamplight, I embrace
my wench, and venus-flogged she bares her face
or looks the other way; and when I leave
I'm no marked man, nor scared that she'll decieve
or that the next's a richer man or better.

You love a wife. You lay aside, to get her,
your garb, your rank's respect, your ring. You shed
your freedom, hooding up your scented head.
Are you not what you seem? You creep and quaver;
your bones are stricken as your passions waver.
The slave who's scourged or slaughtered in the ring,
the box-hid lecher: they're the selfsame thing.
Head pressed against your knees, you lie in doubt
till the accomplice servant lets you out.
Are you not legally in the husband's power?
you and the wife? More wretchedly you cower,
and rightly. She escapes your masquerade.
She doesn't trust you, kissing and afraid.
Deliberately enslaved, you ask for shame
and yield a maddened man your life and name.
You're safe? Then surely saneness now is won.
But no, on death and fear again you run.
Enslaved in infinite toils! what beast, which tore
the net, will trust its body there once more?

'I'm no adulterer,' you swear — and I,
no thief, because I pass the silver by . . .
But lift the bar of fear, what lusts we spy.

Juvenal

I AM ready to believe that when Saturn was King, Chastity dwelt on the earth and was long to be seen there. When a chilly cave provided a meagre home and enclosed in one shade the fire and the house-gods, the cattle and their owners. When a mountain-bred wife made a country-bed with leaves and straw and the skins of the wild beasts who were the family's neighbours. Not a woman like you, Cynthia, whom Propertius loved, or you, Lesbia, whose brilliant eyes were dimmed with tears at a sparrow's death. No, but one well-provided with breasts from which her huge babies might drink rather than suck: one mostly cruder in her ways than even her acorn-belching husband. For men lived very differently then, when all the world was new and the sky had only been freshly strung above – men who, born from the cloven oak or moulded out of clay, knew no parents.

Many survivals of that primeval chastity, or at least a handful of them, may have persisted even when Jove took over the universe. But that was before God's beard was grown, before the Greeks were prepared to swear by somebody else's head: in days when no one feared a thief for his cabbages or apples, but lived without fences round his garden. Then by degrees Justice went into retirement in the heavens above, and with her went Chastity. The two sisters bunked off together.

Yes, Postumus, it's an old old trick, a hackneyed vice to shake the marriage-bed in adultery and make a jok of its guardian spirit. The Iron Age soon ushered in every other sort of iniquity; it was left for the Silver Age to produce the first adulterers.

And yet you're getting ready to marry. You've gone through the first overtures, signed the contract, completed the betrothal. You've put yourself into the hands of the master barber and perhaps you've gone as far as giving the pledge for her finger. Well, once you were comparatively sane. And now, Postumus, now you're going to marry! What Fury, what Hiss of Snakes is driving you dotty? Can you really submit to be a woman's slave while so many halters lie cheap in the shops? while high-up dizzying windows are open for you and the Aemilian bridge rears itself near by? And if, even with such a plentiful choice of suicides you're too fastidious to find one that suits you, why not keep on the way you always have, with a lad who reads you no curtain-lectures, doesn't go on nagging for little presents, and never complains that you're incompetent as a partner in pleasures?

But Ursidius now smiles at the Julian Law with its penalties for adulterers. All his concern is for the rearing of a darling heir. He doesn't mind that he loses the first-rate turtle-dove and the bearded mullet, all the market-dainties that are used by legacy-hunters to captivate the wealthy man with no heirs. Tell me, what would you consider to be impossible, if Ursidius takes a wife? Just think. He, once the most world-famous of adulterers, who has so often hidden himself in the family chest to escape a murderous husband, he is going to stick his idiot head right into the marriage-noose. And what's more, he's looking round for a wife endowed with all the virtues of ancient days!

Hey, you physicians, rush up and bore through his middle vein. Let him blood. What a lovely chap! Fall

down and worship on the threshold of Tarpeian Jove.
Offer up a heifer with golden horns to his wife, Juno,
if you have the remarkable luck to ferret out a matron
with chastity intact. So few are there worthy to handle
the fillets of Ceres. So few, whose kisses would not terrify
their own fathers. Wreathe garlands for the doorposts,
hang thick clusters of ivy across the threshold. Is one
husband enough for Iberina? You might as well ask if
she'd be satisfied with one eye.

'Still, there's a lot of talk going on about a certain
young woman who lives at her father's country villa.'
All right, let her live as quietly in a small country-
town like Gabii, or even Fidenae, and then I'll agree
with what you say about the good influence of the pater-
nal retreat. Yet who will have the face to declare that
no embraces have occurred on lonely mountain-tops or
remote caverns? Are those fabulous lechers Jove and
Mars grown old and nerveless? In all the public
promenades can a single woman be pointed out to you
as worthy of your vow? Scour all the benches of the
show-places: can you find a single female there warm-
ing the seat, whom you could love without the shakes,
without all sorts of misgivings – whom you could pick
out as better than the rest in the rows and rows of
wantons?

While the pretty boy Bathyllus is acting the part of
ravished Leda in the ballet, Tuccia can't hold herself
in, Appula moans and gasps as if she were in the ex-
tremity of love-making, and Thymele is wide-awake to
all the fine points of the game. She may have been a
country-bumpkin a while back, now she knows it all
inside out. Then when the stage scenery is packed away
for the time being and only the law courts are vocal,
the theatres closed and empty with the Megalesian
Games coming so long after the Plebeian, other women

in their sad boredom handle the mask, the thyrsus-wand and the underpants of Accius' out-of-date plays. Urbicus manages to get a laugh by playing the role of Autonoe in the Atellan farces; and Aelia, being hard-up, is infatuated with him. Other ladies pay down a good cash-sum and the comedian agrees to unfasten his brooch-pin. Those who crowd in on Chrysogonus leave him so debilitated that his voice gives out when he tries to sing on the stage. Hispulla has got eyes only for a heavy-part actor. Do you then really imagine that a worthy and respectable citizen like Quintilian will succeed in holding her fancies fast? You marry a wife — so that Echion the harper, or Glaphyrus, or Ambrosius who plays the flute for the ballet, may have the honour of fathering your children. Yes, let's put up the scaffolding for a gladiatorial show, drape the doorposts and the gate with great bunches of laurel, and hoist up the tortoise-shell-inlaid canopy, so that nobly born Lentulus, sitting in the front row, may recognize the man from whom his infant son got his features, the prize-fighter Euryalus.

Hippia was a senator's wife, but that didn't prevent her from chasing after a gladiator all the way to Egypt — to the infamous walls of Alexandria. Even the folk there thought the imperial capital was getting beyond itself in immorality. This woman forgot her home, her husband, her sister; she didn't give a damn for her native land, or, vile wretch, for her crying children. What's more surprising, she was actually ready to go far from the theatres and that admired actor Paris. As a babe she had been nursed in sheer luxury in the down of her father's mansion and a cradle that cost the earth; but now she turned up her nose at all the perils of the sea. Her good name of course she had long ago despised. The loss of that, among the soft cushions of ladies, is very cheaply rated. So, with dauntless bosom, she faced the Tuscan billows and the roaring Ionian sea; she passed through sea after sea. With women like that, if the cause of danger is something reasonable and to their credit, their coward hearts are chilled with icy fear and they can't support themselves on their trembling feet. Only when there is baseness in the dare do they show a brave spirit. Let a husband do the bidding, such a woman complains it's a terrible hardship even to board a ship. Then the bilgewater is intolerable for her poor nerves and the skies spin round her head. But if one of them is following her partner in vice, she has no qualms whatever. The first woman spews all over her husband; the second eats her dinner among the sailors, strolls on the quarter-deck, and thinks it fun to handle the rough ropes.

And what were the charms, the handsome looks, that got under Hippia's skin and made her twitch all over? What did she see in the dog to make up for her nickname as the fencer's whore? Her beloved Sergius had already begun to shave his throat. Badly wounded in the arm, he was looking forward to his discharge. Moreover, his face was disfigured in all sorts of ways. His brow was galled with the helmet; there was a huge wen between his nostrils, and an acrid rheum kept on trickling from his eyes. But what did all this matter? wasn't he a prize-fighter? That made him more beautiful than the legendary lad Hyacinthus. Such was the creature she preferred to her children and her native land, her sister and her husband. It's the bloody steel that the women are enamoured of. Throw this Sergius out of the ring and he'd soon begin to be a mere blob in her eyes.

You're interested in the goings-on of a mere Hippia, a common-or-garden wife? Then turn your eyes to the

Rival of the Gods, the emperor. Listen to what Claudius had to put up with. As soon as his wife saw that he was well asleep, this imperial harlot dared to prefer a ragbag mattress to the royal couch. She took up the hood she wore of nights; she sneaked out of the palace with only one of her girls and with the yellow headgear hiding her black hair; she slipped into the brothel kept warm by an old patchwork quilt, into the empty cell reserved for her. There she took her stand, her breasts bare with their gilded nipples, and assumed the name of Lycisca. She bared the belly of the mother of Prince Britannicus, welcomed every customer with caresses, demanded her price cash down, and gave herself up to as many embraces as she could get. Then when at last the brothel-keeper shut up shop and told the girls to go home, she reluctantly got ready to go and did everything she could to hang on till the last before she closed her cell. Burning still with unsatisfied desire, tired out but raging still for more customers, she went home with sullied cheeks. Smeared with the lamp-smoke, she carried back the stink of the stews to the emperor's pillow.

Do I need to detail the love-philtres, the spells, the poison mixed with the food given to a stepson? The crimes committed in the name of lust are the least reprehensible; worse are the actions into which women are driven by the inescapable impulses of their sex. 'Then how can it be that even by her husband's showing Cesennia is the best of wives?' It's simple. She brought him a fortune. That's the price for his praises of her chastity. It's not arrows from the Venus-quiver that stick in his liver; it's not the Venus-torch that burns him up. It's the dowry that kindles his flames; the arrows are all shot from the money. His wife has bought her freedom; and so, even in her husband's presence, she may exchange love-signals and answer her love-letters. A rich wife, with a husband who loves money, has all the privileges of a widow.

'Why then does Sertorius sigh passionately for his Bibula?' Look at his emotion closely. It's not the wife that he worships; it's the face. Let a wrinkle or two show up, let the skin shrivel and grow flaccid, let the teeth blacken with decay, let the eyes look smaller – 'Pack up your luggage,' the freedman will say without ceremony, 'out you go!' You've become horrible. You blow your nose too often. Come on, be smart about it. Another girl's expected, one whose nose doesn't drip.' But meanwhile she's hot and imperious. She demands from her husband shepherds and sheep from Canusium and elmed vines from Falernum. But that's only a trifle. Next moment every boy that takes her fancy, whole herds of slaves, and anything whatever that she hasn't got in the house and her neighbour has – it all must be bought for her.

Why, in the mid-winter month when the merchant captains are shut up at home and the frost-whitened cottage is packed with the waiting sailors, she insists on getting enormous crystalline vases and myrrhine cups of stupendous size – then an antique adamant, whose history is guaranteed: it's all the more valuable because it was once on Berenice's finger. This ring in long-pas days a barbarian king bestowed on his incestuous love Agrippa gave it to his sister in that land where bare footed kings keep the sabbath holy and the custom to let pigs live out their lives to the full.

'Is there not one, not a single one, among such endle bevies of women, who seems to you a worth-whi match?'

Let her be beautiful, rich, fruitful. Set out along h colonnades her rows of ancestral statues. Let her chaster than one of those Sabine women who rushed out with all their hair down and brought the war to an end. Let her be a very phoenix on earth, as rare as a black swan. Who could bear a wife in whom all excellencies were compacted? I'd rather, any day, have a rustic piece from Venusia than sink under you, Cornelia, mother of the Gracchi, if along with your exalted virtues you include in your dower a supercilious and haughty brow, and counted your house's Triumphs as part of your fortune. Chuck out, I beg you. your Hannibal and Syphax Conquered in his Camp, and do a bunk with your Defeated Carthage!

What decorum of deportment, what beauty, can make up for your wife's perpetual casting of her worth in your teeth? All pleasure in this rare and eminent good is wiped out if, badly spoilt by pride of spirit, it brings with it more bitterness than sweet. Who is so hopelessly uxorious as not to feel a dread of the woman he loudly praises, and to hate her for seven hours out of every twelve? There are certain trifles which can have the effect of crushing a husband. What can be more sick-making than the fact that a woman doesn't consider herself a beauty unless she changes herself from an Italian into a little Greek: transformed from a Maid of Sulmo to a Maid of Athens. Then everything is in Greek – while surely it is more of a disgrace when one of our womenfolk doesn't know her mother tongue. In Greek they express their fears, their angers, their joys, and their worries, and all the innermost workings of their souls. How much farther can they go? They copulate *à la Grecque*. You can pardon such affectation in young girls. But must you as well, with all the wear and tear of eighty-six years, start talking in Greek too? And in an old woman this sort of prattle becomes skittishly lascivious. *Cher ami, ma vie, je t'adore*. She's scattering round in public the sort of epithets that anyone might think you'd just been ejaculating under the bedclothes. Whose propensities wouldn't be excited by such caressing and titillating words? They have all the force of an actual touch. Yet though you, my dear, utter every one of them with more cooing effect than even Haemus or Carpophorus, your face, which blabs the secret of your years, makes all our feathers droop and wilt.

If you aren't even remotely likely to love the woman contracted and given over to you in lawful wedlock, I can't see the least reason why you should marry her – why you should go to the expense of a wedding dinner and of all the bridal cakes you must distribute, at the end of the complimentary visits, to the mob of guests who have come along with guts already well crammed. Not to mention the present you have to make your wife on the first consummating night, a dish heaped high with the gold coins of Domitian. However, if you happen to have such simplicity of character as to be love-struck over your wife and your whole soul is devoted to her alone, bow down your head and prepare your neck to take the yoke. You won't find a single woman who'll spare a man that loves her.

Even if she's in love herself, she takes delight in tormenting and doing her lover down. In consequence a wife is far more disastrous for a man who is likely to make a kindly and proper sort of husband. You'll never be permitted to give a present without the full consent of your wife. If she doesn't agree, you won't be able to sell a single thing, or buy it, unless you win her over. She'll trample on your friendships. That good old pal of many years' long standing she'll shut out from the gate that once saw the first wispy sprouts of his beard. Pimps and circus-trainers have the legal liberty to make their own wills; indeed even gladiators own that privilege; but you'll have your will dictated to you and you'll discover more than one of your rivals mentioned as your heirs.

'Crucify that slave.'

'What is the charge, to deserve such a penalty? What witnesses can you call? who laid the information on which you act? Think and pause. When a man's life is at stake, the deliberations can't be too long.'

'You imbecile – so a slave is a man, eh? Suppose he's done nothing? I will it. I insist on it, see? Let my will stand in place of a reason.'

That's the way she domineers over her husband. But soon she quits the cowed realm; she seeks out new empires and wears holes in her bridal veil. Then she comes fluttering back and wants again to go the routine way into the bed she has scorned. She leaves the recently decorated doors, the tapestry still hung on the walls, and the threshold still green with its festival boughs. The score rapidly mounts. She can nick up her eight husbands in five years. An impressive record to engrave upon her tomb.

Anyhow, you haven't any hope of domestic happiness while your mother-in-law is alive and thriving. She urges her girl to rejoice in fleecing her husband to the last farthing. She teaches her how to compose letters in reply to the seducer, letters without the least flaw of bad manners or of inexperience. She baulks your spies or she bribes them. Then, though her daughter is bursting with health, she calls in an expensive doctor, and tosses off the bedclothes as too oppressive. Meanwhile, the lover, hidden somewhere near by, stands shivering with impatient anticipation. Do you suppose, I ask you, that the mother will train her girl in honest principles, in anything except the ways she herself clings to? Besides, it's highly profitable for a depraved old trot to bring up her daughter along the well-tried lines of her own depravity.

See if you can find a single lawsuit in which a woman doesn't appear as in some way fomenting the whole trouble. If Manilia isn't the defendant, she'll be the plaintiff. Women nowadays even frame bills of indictment without any aid, perfectly ready to dictate even to the highest-standing lawyers the exordium and the topics to be used in their addresses.

We all know the woman's cut of the thick shaggy cloak put on to stop a chill after exertion in the ring; the woman's brand of the oil-wax-and-clay ointment used by gladiators. And who hasn't seen the wounds and scars of the Sword Post, which the sports-girl pricks with her foil as she practises fencing, and attacks with her shield in methodical exercises? Look there. A matron who most emphatically deserves the trumpet at the Floralia. Unless of course she's got some deeper plot brewing in that bosom of hers and is training in dead earnest for the ring. What modesty can you look for in a woman who pops a helmet on her head, acts like a bloody man, and delights in feats of muscle? And yet, in spite of all this, the virago wouldn't want to become a man all over. For how small is a man's pleasure in comparison with what a woman can extract! Still, there'd be a notable pile of things if you were to hold an auction of your wife's gear. Belts and gauntlets and crests and leggings-for-the-left-leg. Or if she goes in for fighting with the net, you'll be in luck when your young wife sells her greaves and armour. Yet these women who'll dress up in heavy sports togs, perspire in the lightest muslin. Their delicate frames are oppressed by a mere yard of sarcenet. What-ho, with what a lot of noise she makes the home-thrusts taught her by the trainer – and what a weight of helmet bows her down, how solidly she sets herself on her haunches, how thickly massed is the roll of her clothes. See if you can hold back your grin when, after taking her equipment off, she picks up the chamber-pot. Tell me, you granddaughters of the grimly moral heroes of our antique chronicles, what actress ever wore such a garb and make-up? and what wife of the old boys ever grunted *hah!* at the practice-post?

The bed which includes a wife is the unceasing scene of brawls, arguments, recriminations. The one thing it's no use for is sleep. That's the time and place when the wife is bitter indeed towards her husband, fiercer than a tigress robbed of her cubs: when, nagged at by her secret guilt, she makes a show of moaning and groaning, of hating the servants or of upbraiding you about some woman she has made up on the spur of the moment – her tears always effective, always ready to gush at a blink, only waiting for her orders as to how they're to flow. You're convinced it's sincere love. You poor hedge-sparrow, plume yourself and kiss the tears away from her lips. Ah, what diatribes and love-letters you'd come across if you were to dip into the writing-desk of that adulteress who can act the jealous part so well.

Suppose her actually caught in the arms of some slave or middle-class gent. 'Yes, what colourable excuse can you think up, Quintilian?'

'I'm quite at a loss. Let the lady speak.'

'Didn't we agree at the outset,' she says, 'that you should do as you pleased and that I also had full right to amuse myself? Make as much noise as you like, and confound heaven and ocean. But I'm mortal.'

Nothing is bolder than these women when found out. They put on a show of resentment and gain courage from the very fact of guilt.

Perhaps you want to know the reason for these monsters and from what source they spring. A humble way of life was what held the Latin women chaste in ancient days. Their lowly roofs were kept from contamination by days of hard toil and nights of brief rest, by hands galled and calloused with working the Tuscan wool, by Hannibal's threatening the City and the husbands' manning the walls and mounting guard at the Colline Tower. Now we are suffering from the effects of prolonged ease. Luxury, more relentless than war, broods over Rome and exacts vengeance for a conquered world. Since Roman poverty was wiped out, no guilt or deed of lust has been lacking. That was how it came about that Sybaris flowed to these Seven Hills, and Rhodes too, and Miletus, and Tarentum crowned with garlands, insolent and wine-flushed.

Money, the nurse of debauchery, was what first brought in alien corrupting manners. Enervating wealth broke the age's morale with filthy high-living. What inhibition does Venus feel when she's drunk? No distinction of head or tail is recognized. She swallows down huge oysters in the very mid-hour of the night, while unguents are foaming, mixed with neat Falernian, and she swigs the big conch-cup. Giddily she feels the ceiling reeling and the table rises up with the lamps doubled in number.

Off with you then, and, knowing what you know, doubt if you can the snort of scorn with which Tullia sniffs the air as she passes by the antique Altar of Chastity – or what Vollatia whispers to her accomplice Maura. Here it is that they set down their litters at night and wet the very image of the goddess with plentiful irrigations, while the chaste moon looks down upon their naughty goings-on – across the scene of which you pass, when morning returns, on your way to call on your important friends.

I can hear the advice that my good friends of ancient

days would offer for dealing with refractory wives: 'Clap on a lock! Shut her up and don't let her out.'

Yes, but who is to guard the guards? Your wife, as crafty as you are, starts with them. And in our age the highest and the lowest are similarly on fire. The woman who wears out the black pavement with her feet is no better than the one who is carried on the shoulders of her tall Syrian litter-slaves.

Ogulnia wants to go in proper state to the Games. So she hires a gown. She hires attendants and a sedan-chair with pillow. She hires female companions and a nurse and a blonde girl to take her messages and the rest of it. Yet all that survives of the family plate, even the very last bits of it, she gives away to well-oiled athletes. Many women live in homes of straitened circumstances, but not one of them owns the modesty and self-control that ought to go hand in hand with being hard-up; not one holds herself in, inside the bounds that her poverty has assigned as her condition in life. Yet men do occasionally look forward and concern themselves with what may be to their later benefit; with the ant as schoolmistress some have even had the sense to feel afraid of cold and hunger catching them up. Woman, however, with her spendthrift ways, doesn't notice at all that her fortune is quickly running away to zero. As if money is a sort of vegetable that will sprout and bloom again from the exhausted coffer, as if the heap from which she takes will replenish itself, she never reckons up the cost of her pleasures.

Some women even take delight in unsoldierly eunuchs. They like soft kisses and cheeks that have given up all hope of a beard. For then they never need bother about abortions. Their pleasure is at its extreme when the creature of their love has been operated on after he reached full manhood, so that nothing much worse has happened than that the surgeon has cheated the barber of his fees. He's a slave, and the woman owns him: she gives the orders for his clipping. Then, catching the eyes of everyone, even those in the distance, he saunters into the Baths and bears comparison with the god who guards our vines and gardens.

If it is singing that excites her, the brooch of none of those chaps who sell their voices to the praetor can stay closed. She can't keep her hands off the instruments; the lyre glints with thickly set jewels all over. She runs over the strings with the busy quill that the womanly Hedymeles used in his performances. She clasps it in her hands; she consoles herself with it and lavishes kisses on the plectrum, which she finds dear for its owner's sake. One of the Lamian clan, a lady of high rank, made offerings of mealcake and wine to Janus and Vesta in the hopes of learning oracularly if Pollio could hope for the Oak Crown at the Capitoline Games and promise it to his lyre. What more could she have done if her husband were lying sick? what more, if the doctors had given up the life of her baby son? She stood before the altar of the gods and felt no shame at veiling her head on behalf of a harper. She went duly through the precribed words and paled as the sacrificed lamb was opened up. Tell me now, I pray, tell me, you most ancient of the gods, Father Janus, do you give answers to such prayers as these? Great indeed must be the leisure of heaven. As far as I can see, there can't be any serious business taking up your thoughts aloft. One woman consults you about comic actors; another wants to bring a tragedian to your notice. The soothsayer will get varicose veins through standing too long.

Still, let your wife rather be musical than dash through the whole City with bold looks and push herself into the gatherings of men, thinking nothing of chatting in her husband's presence with generals in their scarlet cloaks – her eyes unabashed and her breasts well bared. She knows everything that is happening all over the wide world: what the Chinese or the Thracians are up to, the secrets of the stepmother and her son, what adulterer is head-over-heels in love or is in great request among the ladies. She can tell you who it was that got the widow with child, the month in which it was done, the love-language and the exact posture in which each embrace of love is carried out. She's the first to spot the Comet that brings bad luck to the Armenian and Parthian King; and she hangs about the Gates to intercept the reports and the latest news coming in. If there's nothing, she invents a few good stories: Niphates has overwhelmed whole nations in the East; the countryside there is being hopelessly flooded, cities are tottering and the earth is subsiding. She tells this tale in every place of resort to anyone she encounters.

And yet that talkative vice is not so bad. It's far worse that, despite piteous appeals, she'll have her poor neighbours dragged in and slashed in half with the whip. If her heavy slumbers are disturbed by a dog barking, she yells out, 'Get out the clubs at once!' She orders the dog's owner to be beaten first, and then the dog. A horrible sight, with the most frightful face, she goes into the Baths after dark. In the night she commands her bathing vessels and camp to be set in motion. She finds the utmost pleasure in sweating with a hell of a noise: after she has tired out her arms with the ponderous dumb-bells and can't hold them up any longer, and the sly masseur has given her a good rub on every inch of her person. Meanwhile her miserable guests are sinking with hunger and drowsiness. Then at last the lady comes rampaging in, flushed all over and thirsty enough to swill off a whole flagon, which is placed at her foot and filled from a vast jug. She drains a second pint before she touches the food, to make her stomach quite ravenous. And after thus rinsing out her stomach, she returns the wine in a great cascade along the floor. Billows of it gush over the marble pavement and the broad vessel stinks of Falernian. Just as when a long snake glides into a deep cask, she quaffs and she spews. Her husband turns squeamish and feels sick; he closes his eyes and does his best to keep down his heaving bile.

And yet that woman is even more offensive, who, the moment she takes her place at table, launches into panegyrics of Virgil and an apology for the Suicide of Dido — who compares and contrasts one poet with another, dumping Virgil in one side of the scales and Homer in the other. The grammarians give way, the rhetoricians are all silenced, the whole company lies gasping and dumb. Not even a lawyer or the town-crier could get a word in edgeways. Not even another woman. Such a cataract of words comes foaming out, you'd think a forest of brass basons or bells were all being banged at once. After this, nobody need trouble to bring out the trumpets or the sounding brass, as they do to help the moon when she labours under the attack of an eclipse. This woman alone can scare off all the demons of the universe.

The philosopher sets a limit even to things which are good-in-themselves. The woman who wants to seem over-learned and eloquent should wear a tunic that reaches no lower than mid-leg; she ought to sacrifice a pig to Sylvanus, who doesn't accept sacrifices from women; she need only pay a copper and go into the cheapest baths. See to it that the matron who shares your bed doesn't boast a set style of declamation or know how to whirl and hurl in well-rounded sentences the enthymeme curtailed of its premise. Don't let her be acquainted with history books. Instead, see that there are a few things in books that she does actually understand. I hate the woman who keeps poring over and studying Palaemon's treatise on Grammar, who never makes a mistake or gets her sentences tangled up. A woman who is skilled in antiquarian lore and cites poems I've never heard of. A woman who keeps correcting the phrases of her friend as old-fashioned when a man would never notice it. A husband has the right to commit a solecism.

There's nothing a woman won't permit herself, nothing that she considers she ought to be ashamed about, once she has strung emeralds round her throat and inserted big heavy ear-rings in her ears, pulling the lobes right out. Nothing is so insufferable as a rich woman.

Meanwhile her face is horrible to look at, swollen and ridiculous from the huge poultice. Or else it smells profusely of rich Poppaean perfumes and ointments plastered so thick that her wretched husband finds his lips glued up. But to her lover she'll present herself with her skin washed clean. Why then does she choose to be beautiful at home? It's for her lovers that the scents are got ready. It's for them that she buys all the beautifying things that the slender Indian exports to us. At last she uncases her face and strips off the top-layer. She begins to be herself once more, and bathes in the milk of the she-asses that she carries in her train – even if she's sent as an exile to the ends of the earth. But can we call a face something that's overlaid and fomented with so many continually changed cosmetics – something that receives poultices of boiled and damp flour? Can we call it a face or a sore?

It's worth while inquiring to find out just what it is that takes up a woman's time and keeps her busy the livelong day. If her husband has snoozed off with his back turned, there's fine goings-on. The housekeeper is

221

half-murdered. The girls who help with the toilet are stripped for the whipping-block. The Liburnian slave is accused of having come late and is forced to pay the penalty for someone else's sleepiness. Another slave has the rods broken about him. A third bleeds from a whip-flogging. A fourth, from the thongs of cow-hide. Yes, some women pay a regular salary to hangmen for such torture-work. While the blackguard goes on with his lashing, she listens smiling to a friend's chat or lingers fondly over the examination of the broad gold on an embroidered robe. Still the lashings sound. She ponders the entries in her lengthy diary. Still the lashings sound. Then at long last, after the floggers are exhausted, she screams out in a horrible voice, 'Get off with you!' and the inquisition is over.

The rule in her house is as pitiless as the court of a Sicilian Tyrant used to be. Suppose she has arranged a rendezvous with a lover and is anxious to be decked out more flatteringly than usual – she is in a hurry and the lover has already been waiting for her some time in the Gardens or rather near the Chapels of the Isiac bawd. Poor Psecas, with her own locks dishevelled and her bosom bare, is dealing with the lady's hair. 'Why is this curl so high?' Immediately the cow-hide avenges the awful crime of misplacing a hair. What has poor Psecas done? What crime is it of the wretched girl if your own nose happens to displease you?

Another girl, on the mistress's left, draws out the curls, combs and rolls them into a band. The grey-haired housekeeper plays her part in the council-of-charms. She has served her full period as a needle-worker and now has charge of weighing out the wool-tasks; so her opinion will be the first to be asked. Then her inferiors in skill and in years give their vote in order, as if their mistress's good name or life itself were at stake: so great is the problem of ensuring beauty. She builds up her curls into so many tiers; she elevates her head by so many storeys. In front you sink before a tragedy-queen on stilts; at the back you find a dwarf. You feel sure there must be two women. Forgive her, please, if nature has allotted to her an abbreviated back, and if without the support of high-heeled shoes she dwindles below a pigmy maid, so that she has to lift on tiptoe and give a jump to get a kiss. But meanwhile there's no thought whatever for the husband. Not a word of her beggaring expenditure. She lives as if she were merely a neighbour of his. The only respect in which she shows her close connexion with him is in the hate she feels for his friends and servants, and in the crushing inroads that she makes on his purse.

But look! the worshipping mob of demented Bellona and the Mother of the Gods burst into the house, together with the great flabby eunuch – a face to be revered by his dirty inferior – who long past emasculated himself with a broken potsherd. The hoarse crowd and the guttersnipe drummers yield place to him as he struts, his cheek covered with the Phrygian tiara. In a booming voice he bids the lady fear the advent of September and the gusts of autumn, unless she first purifies herself with a hectacomb of eggs and presents him with her discarded robes coloured like late vine-leaves. Then, he says, whatever unforeseen or terrible dangers are hanging over her will pass into the cloths and expiate all her sins of the year in one moment. She is to break the ice and plunge into the river in the winter's depth, or dip thrice in the Tiber at early dawn and bathe her shrinking head within its eddies – proceeding to crawl out and go on bleeding knees, naked and shivering, over the whole Field of Mars. And if white Io bids her, she is to travel to the farther ends of Egypt and fetch back water from scorching Meroe for sprinkling on the Temple of Isis which rears close by the Election Grounds. And she believes that the warning has been given her by the very voice of the Goddess. Such as hers are obviously the souls fit to hold converse with the immortals by night!

That man reaps the highest honour, who, hemmed round by his linen-garbed flock and a throng with shaven heads uttering lamentations, scampers to and fro and personates the grinning god Anubis. He it is who supplicates for forgiveness when his wife insists on being made love to on days marked for abstinence and a heavy penalty is exacted for violation of the snow-white sheets. O yes, and the silver serpent was seen to nod its head! His are the tears and his the meditated mumblings which win Osiris over not to refuse his pardon for her sin – on getting the bribe of a fat goose and a thin cake. When he has taken his leave, a Jewess comes in, all of a tremble. She has left her basket and hay, and whispers her prayer into the woman's secret ear – the interpretess of Jerusalem, the potent priestess of the Tree, the reliable go-between from the highest heavens. She gets her hand crossed with money, though meagrely enough: Jews will sell you any dreams you want for a mite of a coin. The soothsayer of Armenia or Commagene, pawing at the yet-reeking liver of a dove, assures the woman that her lover will be her slave or promises her the broad inheritance of some wealthy man without children. He pokes into the bosoms of chickens and the bowels of a puppy; sometimes even into those of a child – and then no doubt he'll turn informer and blame the woman who paid him.

But female confidence in Chaldeans is even greater. Whatever the astrologer tells them, they take as something straight from the horse's mouth, from God Himself. Yet at Delphi the oracles are dumb now, and complete ignorance about the future is the punishment laid on the human race.

Be sure to shun, even for a casual encounter, any woman in whose hands you see a calendar as thumbed and rubbed as a bit of scented amber. A woman who, instead of consulting fortune-tellers, is herself consulted. A woman who, when her husband is off for his military service or on a visit to his home, will refuse to go with him if she finds the astrological computations are adverse. When she has a fancy to ride out to the first milestone, she extracts the lucky hour for it from her book. If the corner of her eye itches when she rubs it, she inspects her horoscope before calling for an appropriate ointment. If she lies sick abed, she won't take food at any hour but that which her astrologer has laid down. If she be of slight means, she'll cross the space on both sides of the circus-pillars, draw lots, and hold out her brow and her hand to the obsequious palm-reader. The rich call in some Phrygian prophet, some Indian juggler expressly hired, some pundit of the stars, or some aged hobbler who specializes in purifying public spots struck by lightnings. The poor folk troop along to the quacks in the circus or on Tarquin's Rampart. The woman, who lacks any golden necklace to display, goes and asks in front of the obelisks and the dolphin columns if she will turn down the tapster and wed the old-clothes man.

One scoundrel offers spells of magic to a wife. Another sells her love-potions from Thessaly to cloud her husband's brains and bring him down to the indignity of slippers. That's the way you're reduced to dotage. That's how you acquire your dizzy moments, your peculiar habit of forgetting what you've just done. Yet even that would be tolerable, as long as you were not sent raving mad as well.

Women hate their husbands' bastards. Well, that's what you'd expect and excuse. But now it is thought quite the correct thing to kill even their husbands' sons by a former marriage. Beware, all you that are under age and own a large estate. Watch over your lives. Don't trust a single dish. The rich meats steam livid with venoms that your mother has mixed. If she brings you anything by her own hands, make sure that someone else has a sup first. Let your school-tutor, in terror of his life, taste all your cups.

You'll say I've made the whole thing up. Satire is borrowing the Tragic Buskin, eh? I only wish that what I say was a wild fable. But listen to Pontia over there. She shouts at the top of her voice, 'I did the deed. I admit it. I prepared the aconite for my own children. You've found it in the food. I did it all.'

'What, you most vicious of all known vipers, did you kill off two at one meal? Did you kill two at a blow?'

'I'd have killed seven if there'd been seven of them!'

Then let us credit all that the tragedy-writers recount of ferocious and merciless heroines. I believe every word of it. The ladies did things that were monstrous even for those crude days. Only they didn't do it for money. That's the unique achievement of our own day.

SOURCES

1. Proem to Book I
2. Poem 16
3. Epigrams, iv. 71
4. *Apologia* of Apuleius
5. Elegies, iii.13 (ii.22a)
6. Poems 5, 7
7. *Satiricon,* 132
8. *Amores,* ii. 4
9. *Pro Caelio,* 15-6, 20
10. Odes, i. 5
11. *Amores,* ii.11
12. Elegies, ii.4. 29 ff
13. *Noctes,* i. 8
14. *Amores,* iii.2
15. Cicero, *Epistulae ad Familiares,* viii.7
16. Poem 13
17. *Amores,* i.5
18. *Poëtae Latinae Minores* iv, *Anthologia Latina,* nos. 213, 215, 214
19. *Mostellaria,* ii, 2 ff
20. *C.I.L. (Corpus Inscriptionum Latinarum)* iv. 5296; M.della Conte, *Amori e Amante di Pompei Antica* (Pref. 1958) p. 70
21. Generally printed at the end of Tibullus, Book iv
22. *Amores,* i. 11, 12
23. *Pervigilium Veneris:* see for ex. J. W. Mackail in the Loeb *Catullus*
24. Satires, xv.5 (G)

25. *Satiricon,* 111-2
26. Epigrams, v.45, vi.23, x.84, x.8, x.9, viii.35, viii.53 (to Catulla), xi.21
27. *Against Verres,* ii, 24-27
28. Poem 6
29. Cited Quintilian, iv.2.123
30. Poem 55
31. *Philippic* ii.31
32. *Ep. ad Fam.* ix.26
33. Odes, i.19
34. *Amores,* i.4
35. Odes, i.13
36. *Miles Gloriosus,* opening of Act i
37. Sat. iv.10 (G.)
38. From his play with this title: E. H. Warmington, *Remains of Old Latin,* ii (Loeb) 1936 p. 98
39. See Della Conte's book cited for no. 20 above; also his *Case ed Abitanti di Pompei,* 1954; and J. Lindsay, *The Writing on the Wall*
40. E. Diehl, *Vulgärlatinische Inschriften*
41. Poem 20 *(P.L.M. 93)*
42. *Mercator,* 405 ff
43. *Noctes,* xv.10
44. Epigram 89
45. See refs. for no. 39 above
46. *Amores,* ii.10
47. Golden Ass, ix.24-25
48. Odes, i. 27
49. *Nat. Hist.,* vii.3
50. Priapea 50

51. *Amores,* ii.7-8
52. Odes, iii.15
53. *Pro Plancio,* 12
54. *Copa,* in the Virgiliana
55. *Golden Ass,* ii.5-10
56. Poem 32
57. *Noctes,* vi.9-12
58. Ciciero, *De Oratore,* ii.68-69
59. *Fasti,* ii.523 ff
60. Eclogue 3
61. Diehl, as for no. 40 above
62. Poem 71
63. *Anthologia Latina,* Reise, 329, 358, 368
64. *Satiricon,* 65-69 and 74-77
65. Elegies, i.5 49 ff
66. *Julius Caesar,* 49
67. The same, 49 and 51
68. Poems 57, 43, 41, 29
69. *Augustus,* 69-70
70. Sat. xvii.1 (G.)
71. End of iv.8
72. Poem 42
73. *Satiricon,* 6-8
74. Epode 12
75. *Amores,* i.14
76. Poems 37, 39
77. Epig., xi.66
78. Poem 23
79. *Epist.* 97
80. Poem 97

81. Caligula 36
82. Priapea 32, 57
83. Catullus 93, 104, 92
84. Elegies, v.8
85. *Amores,* ii.5
86. *Miles Gloriosus,* ii.2
87. O. Ribbeck, *Scaenicorum Romanorum Poesis Fragmenta* ii (3rd ed.) 1897
88. Opening of iii.17
89. *Anthologia Latina,* no. 277
90. *Miles Gloriosus,* act iii, earlier section
91. Elegies, ii.8
92. *Amores,* ii.2
93. *Noctes,* xi.8.9
93. *Fescenninum de Nuptiis Honorii Augusti* iv. 16 ff; *Satiricon,* 24-6; *Silvae,* i.2.268 ff
95. *Amores,* ii.15
96. Poem 61
97. Sat. ii.7 46 ff
98. The Sixth Satire

INDEX OF AUTHORS

References are to the numbers of the items.